Leonie
HER AUTOBIOGRAPHY

LEONIE FORBES
as told to Mervyn Morris

LMH PUBLISHING LIMITED

Editor: Kim Robinson-Walcott
Cover Design: Sanya Dockery

Published by LMH Publishing Limited
Suite 10-11
Sagicor Industrial Complex
7 Norman Road
Kingston C.S.O., Jamaica
Tel.: (876) 938-0005; 938-0712
Fax: (876) 759-8752
Email: lmhbookpublishing@cwjamaica.com
Website: www.lmhpublishing.com

Printed in the USA   ISBN: 978-976-8202-99-4

NATIONAL LIBRARY OF JAMAICA CATALOGUING-IN-PUBLICATION DATA
Forbes, Leonie
    Leonie : her autobiography / Leonie Forbes as told to Mervyn Morris

    p. : ill. ; cm

ISBN 978-976-8202-99-4

1. Forbes, Leonie, 1937 -   2. Actresses – Jamaica – Biography
3. Autobiography
I. Morris, Mervyn   II. Title

792.026092   - dc 22

for Alma MockYen,
Muriel Amiel
and my children

Contents

Acknowledgements   vii
Preface   ix

Tracking Family   *1*
School   *11*
Beginning in Radio   *17*
Theatre Training   *23*
Love and Marriage   *35*
Continuing in Radio   *45*
Australia   *49*
Divorce and Marriage   *59*
Dreams and Visions   *67*
Return to JBC   *75*
Doing *Old Story Time*   *83*
Some Other Challenges   *99*
Reflections   *123*

Appendix 1: From Leonie's Resumé   135
Appendix 2: From Leonie's Review Scrapbook   145

Acknowledgements

Leonie Forbes thanks everybody who has helped; especially
Ruth Ho Shing, Karen Amiel and Ann Marie Stewart.

Mervyn Morris gratefully acknowledges the assistance of
a University of the West Indies Mona Campus Fellowship,
and thanks Kim Robinson-Walcott and Alma Mock Yen
for detailed comments on a draft.

Preface

I have enthusiastically admired many performances by
Leonie Forbes, and have expressed my admiration in
print. So, although I did not know her well, I was pleased
to be asked if I would help with the autobiography she
wanted to write. I said yes, and she began to talk her life.
Prompted minimally, she gave up information well beyond
her involvement in theatre. I was captivated by her story
and her way of telling it. What I have done, essentially, is
organize and edit her recall.

She talks about her formation, about joys and difficul-
ties in her personal life, about being intuitive, about the
complexity of her beliefs. She talks about God, love, relationships, coincidence, dreams and the paranormal. She
traces her career in broadcasting. She discusses theatre
training and some of the challenges she has faced as an
actor. She tells of some uncanny moments – as the mother
of Judas in *The Rope and the Cross*, for example, and as Ojuola

in *The Gods Are Not to Blame*. She talks in detail about playing Miss Aggy in *Old Story Time*.

As an actor she is remarkable not only for technical facility but for the emotional richness she can communicate in demanding roles. There is a profound relation between her life experience and her most memorable performances. As she tells us, "When you suffer emotional trauma you take the energy from the pain and the loss and the confusion or whatever it is, and turn it right around." In *Leonie* a complicated human being proffers facets of herself.

— Mervyn Morris

Leonie

Stanislavski . . . demands that you use everything that happens to you. If something hurts you, once you've gotten over it you sit down, review it and file it so that if you need it it is there. If something wonderful happened to you, you remember not just the feeling of something wonderful happening but exactly how you reacted, what you felt, what you did.

Leonie, age 4

Chapter One

Tracking Family

I was born in Kingston, at Jubilee Hospital, in 1937, the 14th of June. From little bits and pieces I've been able to gather from older members of the family, my natural mother, Hermine Samuels, was a teenager and I was a terrible mistake; so that her sister, who was a little bit older, and married, brought her from St Elizabeth into Kingston to await the arrival of the little blessing. My mother's sister – Aunt G – took me home from the hospital. I went home with her and her husband, and I was raised as their child.

When I was born Aunt G was living at Princess Street. I can remember an upstairs place; downstairs was a furniture shop which her husband ran, and we lived upstairs. I remember another place, corner of East Queen Street and Wildman Street. Again an upstairs place – downstairs he had a restaurant and something else – and we lived upstairs. From there we moved to Slipe Road, just down the road from Carib Theatre, and I remember walking through a little track at the side of the road to go to Mico Practising School. After that, I went to my grandparents in St Elizabeth.

My great-grandfather – my grandmother's father – lived in the hills between Maggotty and Ipswich, two railway stations. He was a huge man, very tall, and everybody called him Puppa. My grandmother's name was Samuels, and she married a Samuels; but she was black Samuels and my grandfather was sort of light-skinned Samuels. They were Seventh Day Adventists; and by the time I came along they were leading citizens in the area, with a little bit of property. When Pastor visited the district he would stay at my grandparents' house, and the rest of the people of the district would bring them their little baskets of what-not. I remember Pastor as a tiny little man.

I can remember one of the first things I ever did wrong. Pastor was down for Baptism and Holy Communion. I turned up at my grandparents' home when they weren't expecting me, and they put my grandfather's merino on me to sleep in, and I came out to show Pastor and ask him if he liked my nightie. The family got very upset.

One of the things I remember about going between Ipswich and Kingston was that every time my adopted mother – Aunt G – and her husband had a fight I got shipped somewhere, either to the country by train or to another aunt (whether courtesy aunt or real aunt) or some cousin till it blew over, then I would be back.

Aunt G's first husband (Uncle John) was Jonathan Forbes. That's where my Forbes comes from (my father's name was Vassell). Uncle John was involved in the Salvation Army, and his business and his lodge. I remember going into Bramwell Booth Hall with him and a man called Joseph who used to lick the Jesus out of the drums. I remember Uncle John, a large man, taking me for ice cream. I remember the first doll he gave me — I had it until I must have been around fourteen and a cousin mashed it up. Uncle John used to like when Aunt G dressed me in a frilly dress and made the little drop curls in my hair and put in the pretty bow. Aunt G was a very good dressmaker and she made me beautiful clothes.

When I was five or six, Aunt G and Uncle John split up, they just couldn't make it anymore. I stayed on with Aunt G. The first place we lived after we moved out was on Church Street, at the very top. After Church Street we went to King Street, nearly opposite the first health clinic built mainly for schoolchildren. There had been a dump there before. From King Street we went to Portland Road; and I stayed there until I left school, in my teens.

Aunt G's second husband, Roderick Wedderburn (Uncle Weddie), who was originally from Cuba, was not as outgoing as Uncle John, but in his own quiet way he was always there and you had to behave. He ended up as stationmaster of Kingston, and this was because of Aunt G who was always pushing him. She would say, "Learn to drive, Weddie, a man must learn to drive. Weddie, you must get a car, forget the bicycle, car is the coming thing, you must get it." And she'd be there behind him like that. I can remember a friend of hers saying, "But why are you doing that for him? Why you don't do it for yourself?" She said, "Me fine. Me is perfectly all right. You mek him go and learn these things." He migrated to the United States for a few years and did very well. When he retired and came back home, he became more talkative.

Aunt G had no children of her own, but she was always looking after other people's children. When I was nineteen and had just started working at the university, I went to see her one weekend. Uncle Weddie, who at that time was in charge of the Bodles railway station, said, "I have a surprise for you." Then I saw Aunt G come off the train with a little baby, the epitome of malnutrition, just a big head and a tummy. I said, "Where you going with that?" She said, "Shet yu mout! One little month of good food and a little love and you'll be surprised!" That was Aunt G. People passing along the road and she would call them and play with their baby and find out if the baby was eating properly. She raised a number of children. Sometimes I'd see her cry — because, as soon as the kids had enough clothes to put in a suitcase, the parents would come back for them, and she'd get terribly upset and say, "I never woulda tek another one!" But give her a couple of months, she'd find another one.

I used to see my natural mother every time I went to the country where my grandmother was. I can even remember a bit of my mother's wedding: the procession up to the church and then the procession back to the yard where the booths were set up. There is that memory somewhere — walking up the side of that hill, and being very small and not being in the limelight but certainly not left out of things.

I couldn't have been more than five. I seem to remember this little person sort of trundling behind everybody. Over the years my mother would come to Kingston when she had to shop for her house. Almost every time she had a new baby!

Before I went off to Australia in 1968, I went looking for Uncle John. By this time he had businesses on Oxford Street near to Coronation Market — bar and furniture shop and restaurant and what not. I went, and he seemed so pleased. It was Good Friday. We went to pick him up and brought him to my home, and he met my children. He said it was a pity I was going off to Australia but that when I came back everything would be fine. He implied that he too was sorry that there had been this long period when we were not in touch. But, towards the end of '69, some boys came into his bar one evening and bought some Wink, and he said, "Don't leave with the bottles," and they shot him and he died. I got the cable in Australia.

Maybe Uncle John and his Salvation Army work and his taking me to some of the meetings were pointing me towards theatre. Ed "Bim" Lewis told me it was Uncle John who had helped set him up in his theatre business, and that he knew Ranny Williams ("Mas Ran"). Bim said, "Is your father Jonathan help me go into this thing." By then Uncle John was dead, I couldn't ask him anything.

I remember seeing my father, twice. Once, my mother was in Kingston and she took me to a photographer, and on the way she turned down a road and took me to this nice gentleman — Indian extraction, "coolie-royal" — and there were people all around him. All I remember is peering over the counter, and he gave me a bag of sweets and five shillings which my mother took. Then some years later, when I was living with Aunt G at Slipe Road, I remember being locked into the outside bathroom, and I'm saying, "Why they locking me in the toilet?" I heard these voices outside, so I climbed up and peeped over the top, and I saw a man's legs disappearing up the stairs. And Aunt G was saying, "Mi no know weh yu come here fa. Mi no tell yu nobody no waan see yu? She no waan nutten from yu!" I gather that was my father. It was his last visit. I gather that it was when I was on one of those trips to the country that he died. I must have been eight or nine. And nobody ever said anything more about him.

I've come to realize that Aunt G, who had seemed so kind, was also controlling, manipulative, and jealous of my birth mother who was fair-skinned and bright. When you're very young you're not quite sure what's happening. I couldn't understand why my natural mother was so distant. It seemed to me at different points in my life as if she resented me for something — perhaps because my arrival had disrupted her studies or other plans she had had. I've come to understand that Aunt G kept me away from my birth mother and her family. She wouldn't allow my mother to bring me gifts or have anything to do with me. I was sixteen before I met some of my brothers and sisters.

One of my sisters lives in Toronto. In 1988 when *The Rope and the Cross* went to Toronto, my mother flew up from

New York to see me perform. At the end of the performance my sister came backstage to say, "She's out front." Wasn't willing to come backstage — too many people, she said — but she waited for me to come out. As I was walking towards her, she got up and she seemed so pleased. To me it seemed the most natural thing in the world to just hug her, and I did. For a split second I thought, *This is where I belong, this is what has been missing*, a sort of spontaneous show of affection or something. When I got back to the hotel that night I had a good cry. I was thinking, *I have never known this, so why should I miss it? Why didn't I have it before? Couldn't I have had it from somebody else? Did I have to do without it all this time?*

My mother is a very religious lady, a Seventh Day Adventist, so it was good that she saw me in *The Rope and the Cross*. She said she thought the performance was wonderful, but I wasn't really listening for that. She said, "Imagine, you are fifty years old" — I was nearly fifty-one — "fifty years, my first child, and till now I haven't hugged her, have hardly spoken to her." And then the following afternoon we had a good old chat at my sister's. I was asking tons of questions. I asked her, "What was my father like?" She kept saying he was a very nice person, kind and so on, but she wouldn't give me very much. Maybe it was painful. But then one gathered that her coolness, her distance from me, her seeming not to like me at all, or to want me around, had nothing really to do with me or even her feelings as my mother. When she came to see me at Aunt G's she wasn't allowed to play with me. When she sent stuff for me, it would be thrown away or presented as something from Aunt

G. She was not supposed to have anything to do with me. So the time when she took me to the photographer and I saw my father, that was a *tief-out*. She said that after a while she found a way to deal with it, which was to just leave me alone. Consequently there were a lot of things about my family which I was not told. I didn't know, for example, that my grandfather was a tremendous musician. Apparently from about the end of November each year nobody saw him until after Christmas. He played the violin and the banjo, and he and his brothers performed all over the place. I learnt that I had brothers and sisters who sang beautifully and loved to act, and so on. Aunt G is a very good mimic, and in recent years I am realizing so is my mother. And two of my sisters have a kind of sixth sense, like me — have dreams that predict. I found all those things fascinating, and I thought, *My God, I wonder how I would be if I had known all this before, instead of seeing myself as this lone throwaway in the desert fighting my way through.*

In 1992 one of my brothers was hit down and killed, and there was a family gathering. There were the five girls and my mother and Aunt G. I said, "Come, Mom," in front of Aunt G. It was amazing to see myself among these women. *Sister. Sister. And that's my mother. And that's mi other mother, who is Aunt G.* Suddenly I belonged to a whole big group, something I didn't know much about. I won't say I missed it, or that I longed for it, but I wondered about it. My mother had fourteen children, nine are alive. I have nieces and nephews that I have never seen, I don't know their names, if I pass them on the road I won't know I had. Sometimes this bothers me. And then I think, *That's life.* I have brothers who are nice men. One especially seems to be making an effort to connect: he calls and he will pop by. Others I see on occasion. Most of them live abroad.

I try to keep in touch with my mother, and to see her whenever I'm in New York. Until she began to slip away — she has Alzheimer's now — she was always a joy to visit. When I walked into the room, her face would light up. And on the phone she would be full of laughter, joking about her glaucoma, high blood pressure and arthritis. She would say, "Lord, mi love, the arthritis hook me up. I lie down yuh see, and I pray, and as soon as it ease I get up and I put on mi clothes and I gallop outa street and do what I have to do and come back." And she would laugh.

Leonie and friend, age 15

Chapter Two

School

The first school I went to was St Luke's Nursery School, near to where I was living (with Aunt G and Uncle John) at Slipe Road. After that, when I was with my grandparents in St Elizabeth, I attended Merrywood Elementary School. I remember my first morning there. Miss Juliet talked about "A", and when she said, "Try to write it," I didn't know she meant that I should write it on my slate. I went to the blackboard and, because I was stretching up to try and form the letter, the other children could see *mi baggie*. They giggled and I was most upset. That was my first day. After that it was all right.

When I came back in Kingston, I went to Mico Practising School. Then, because we moved, there was a brief spell at the North Street Seventh Day Adventist School, then at St George's Girls' School.

Then I was back in the country for a while with my grandparents. I was a very good mimic and liked to make friends laugh, so it seemed natural, one day, to let them dare me to take on Mother Jane, a blind lady living near the church. I pretended to be Mother Jane's daughter from America — accent and all. Told her I was just back from the States and would get her bread and sugar and saltfish and whatever else she needed. I don't know if she believed me, but I thought I'd die when she raised her hands and explored my face. I froze. Word got back to my grandmother and I got the beating of my life. She made me clean out my savings pan to buy the things I'd promised Mother Jane. "When you make a promise you must keep it." I've never forgotten that lesson, nor the feel of Mother Jane's hand roaming my face.

When I came back from the country I went to Love Lane Junior School, because at that time if you didn't you couldn't get into the Kingston Senior School. At Kingston Senior School I had a form master called Mr Keane, the handsomest and sexiest gentleman in the world. I used to walk a mile and a half out of my way to pass his yard, just to see if I see him, just to look and run. Big crush! On a Friday morning we used to have a class concert — you could sing, or tell a story, or dance, or recite a poem. On this particular morning, we hadn't prepared anything, apart from some tired songs and dance, and Mr Keane decided he would read a poem to us. It was "Sohrab and Rustum" by Matthew Arnold. I remember Mr Keane almost doubled over, no proper posture or anything, but we were captivated by his voice, and half of us were in tears. I never ever forgot that reading.

I also remember Louise Bennett's visit to Kingston Senior School. She was slim at the time. She worked with us on the alphabet song. I was very much impressed with the lady, and the way she moved and the way she could just stand up there and make us want to do things.

In 1951 I went to Excelsior on a half scholarship. Aunt G didn't like me being involved in sport. I used to have to dodge her to get to training sessions and sometimes even to an athletic meet. I remember once I was on the Excelsior track team and she gave me worm medicine — followed by "salt physic" (Epsom salts) — the night before the big event at Sabina Park. When I got up the following morning, I was so weak I couldn't even stand up. That was the end of my athletic prospects.

When the music teacher decided we should do an operetta I was first at the auditions. Aunt G was pleased; she liked me to perform, liked me to stand out from the crowd. I think I may have begun performing simply to please her. I'm not quite sure when performing became something I did for myself rather than for her.

Except for health science, Excelsior offered no science subject at the time. I didn't like Latin, and I dropped it. I was good at English language, and pretty good at maths, Spanish and English literature. I was always near the top of my class. The year I came fifth, Aunt G was livid. Even when I was first, there was always something she would quarrel about. She would look at the report and say, "But you history teacher say you could get better marks," or,

"You geography teacher say you could do better." She was never satisfied.

We didn't have the funds for me to go on to sixth form and prepare for the Higher School Certificate; nor, for that matter, to continue the music lessons I had started with Mrs Vidal-Smith. Aunt G tried, but the money couldn't stretch. She decided that I had to be properly equipped for something, so she said, "Well, you might at least learn to type and do shorthand and then you could get a secretarial job or something." I wasn't sure I wanted that, but it sounded better than the civil service. So off I went to Durham Commercial College at the bottom of South Camp Road; and I got connected with the YWCA on North Street so I could learn office routine.

Those people at the YWCA – Leila Beckett and Carmen Lusan and their staff – were thorough and they trained me well. That was the platform from which everything – the rest of my life, so to speak – was launched.

Leonie, age 14

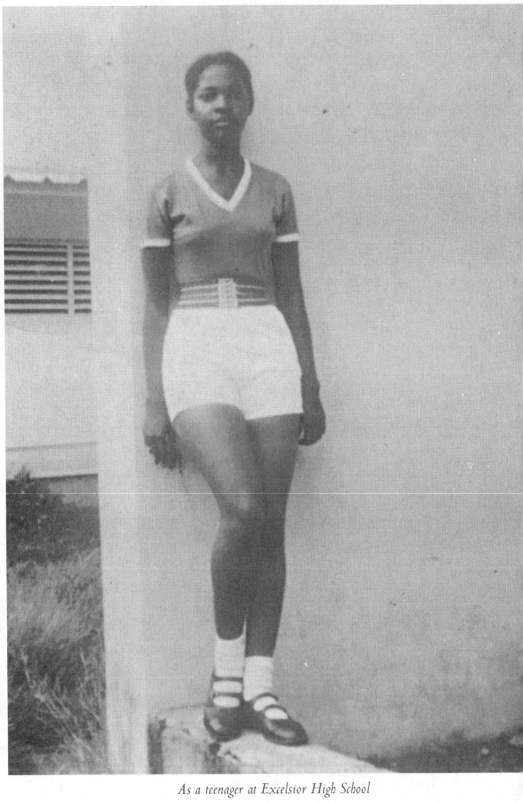

As a teenager at Excelsior High School

Chapter Three

Beginning in Radio

*I*n 1955, I went to the Extra Mural Department to work as a typist for Philip Sherlock — he later became Sir Philip. I was coming straight from training sessions at the YWCA where Leila Beckett and Carmen Lusan had taught me office routine. Mr Sherlock's secretary was going on leave and he needed somebody to type for a couple of weeks, so Miss Beckett sent me as the temporary replacement. I remained with the Extra Mural Department for five years because the Radio Education Unit (REU) had begun and I was shifted over to work with its head, Hugh Morrison. As the secretary to the REU, I typed scripts for adult education programmes that were circulated by the West Indies Broadcasting Service (WIBS) and other stations in the Caribbean.

One afternoon — in 1956, I think — somebody didn't turn up for an REU recording. Mr Morrison said, "Read this out loud," and I did. He said, "Fine. You're coming to the studio with us." That was how my broadcasting career began. Soon afterwards I recorded a *Spanish by Radio* series with Mr Morrison, in which I played his niece Lolita. The series was broadcast on RJR and also did the Caribbean circuit. Shortly after that came the Government Information Service (GIS) programmes with Carey Robinson, in which he would dramatize government messages: for example, about the consequences of praedial larceny and what the laws were and how to make contact with various social services. Then in 1959 the Jamaica Broadcasting Corporation (JBC) began and a radio producer named Robin Midgely came from the British Broadcasting Corporation (BBC) to help set up JBC's Radio Theatre. I got parts in a number of his media productions. I read some poetry as well.

Then I learnt that JBC was looking for announcers. People such as Dick Pixley, Erica Allen, Adrian Robinson and Reggie Carter were already on board. Encouraged by Dick Pixley, I went for an audition. A fortnight later I got a call from the general manager's secretary asking me to come in the following morning at eleven. I got time off and made my way to Half-Way-Tree. Captain William Strange, the JBC general manager, said quietly, "The job is yours if you can start on Monday."

I raced back to the university and told Mr Morrison. He said, "Jolly good. I've been telling them to pay you more." He helped me write my resignation from the REU and took it over to the Registry. On Monday morning I was at JBC. I kept up my work in radio theatre. Most people didn't know I was to be an announcer until my training period was over and they heard me on the air giving time checks and information about the weather.

The training period lasted a month. I worked in the studio with some of the senior announcers, reading commercials, reading the news, eventually being allowed to handle a programme on my own. I got my first speech lesson as a result of my first morning on air. Mrs Rita Coore called up and said, "Darling, you have a lovely little voice but you not talking right. Come and see me." I went, and she gave me a little book, and she explained some of the things I was doing wrong.

Standards were high at JBC. You didn't dare arrive five minutes before your shift. You didn't dare go into the studio without a script even if you only had a fifteen-minute slot to cover. We had to research our programmes thoroughly. We couldn't have a day off and not come in with something, whether it was a taped interview or just a simple greeting from somebody out in the country somewhere. The staff was constantly reminded that Kingston wasn't Jamaica as far as radio was concerned. Announcers had to go out of town. I can remember that technical operators, on their days off, would get a vehicle and we'd take a stack of tapes and head out along the St Thomas road and come around by Manchioneal and Port Antonio and back through Junction. Or another time we'd go to Williamsfield and Santa Cruz or along the north coast. We had to hunt for little things to make our programmes interesting. We'd talk to older people like the Jeffrey-Smith sisters in Spanish Town who could tell us when King's House in Spanish Town burnt down — you'd put the microphone down, ask one question and all three would give you the reply. We had hours and hours of tape recordings which we would edit into five-minute presentations. We heard about when the cholera ship arrived, when the first seaplane came to Jamaica and the great trip they took into Kingston to see these events, and when the price of silk was penny-ha'-penny a yard. Wonderful recollections!

I learnt a lot from the earliest JBC people. One watched and listened and learnt as much as one could and then tried to apply it. This doesn't happen so much in radio nowadays – everybody is a star overnight.

My first little programme was fifteen minutes long, called *Dip and Fall Back*. I had to get information on some of the other islands – for instance, what we call *naseberry* in Jamaica is called *sapodilla* somewhere else, and what we call *guinep* is *ackee* somewhere else. That sort of thing. We weren't allowed to ad lib, we had to write everything down – sometimes you'd feel Adrian's eye on the back of your neck in the studio and he'd come in and say, "Let me see what you just said," and you'd say, "Let you see what I just said?" He'd say, "Yes. You're supposed to write it down." So we travelled with our notebooks and our pencils and there was a book to log things. But it was exciting because we had a lot of outside broadcasts, and for me it was quite an experience standing there in front of all those people (it was not the same as acting in a play). JBC used to have weekly variety shows from the Carib Theatre or the nearby Regal Theatre and a stage show where the Top 10 was announced. At that time JBC had an orchestra and I was learning to play the xylophone and drums — officially though, I acted as an announcer, sharing the honours with Erica Allen. I was challenged once by the audience who only wanted to hear their Top 10, not the coconut oil commercial from Seprod — who sponsored the segment — and I broke out with, "Cho man, nuh gwan so! How we gwine pay for the show if we doan do the commercial?" They roared with laughter and didn't give any more trouble.

At that time too, JBC was involved with fundraising for charities. *Nuggets for the Needy* was the programme by which we solicited donations. It was a successful production and lasted many, many years. I remember somebody paying five pounds to see me walk up the steps in a hobble dress. Contributions were made for all sorts of things, serious and frivolous.

Carmen Manley was writing our first soap opera, *Shadows of the Great House*. I used to earn a little extra money typing the scripts for her, and occasionally she'd give me an incomplete character and say, "Precious is the character you play. Fill it out as an exercise." She and Alma Mock Yen gave me a lot of guidance in scriptwriting, so by the time I typed the script I had the Precious character delineated.

Before returning to the BBC, Robin Midgely insisted I do an audition for the Royal Academy of Dramatic Art (RADA) because a scholarship might be available. I asked Cecil Watt to record the audition tape I planned to send to England. I filled out the application form, supplied photographs of myself, packaged them neatly and delivered them to Midgely who willingly acted as courier. I was excited at the possibilities but nonetheless soon forgot about it all, convincing myself that to get to England to study drama and theatre was a mere pipe dream.

About six months later, RADA accepted my application on the basis of the recording, and granted me a scholarship to study in London. But the scholarship covered tuition only. It was left to me to deal with living expenses and general subsistence. I searched right, left and centre for a solution. It came from Peter Orr, who was attached to the British Council office in Kingston. He helped me get a British Council bursary. I left for London in 1961.

Chapter Four

Theatre Training

*I*n England the acting course is two years, and if you want to teach as well it would be three years. But if Stanislavski is to be believed — and I do believe him — you don't begin to say anything training-wise until after about fifteen years. At the better acting schools that I know of, it's a two-year course and it's pretty rough because they not only deal with a straight modern or contemporary technique but usually — at least in England — we had to deal with Shakespeare, the Restoration plays, Chekhov, Brecht and all that, and then we had to study method acting and Laban theory and all that.

I found Laban theory most valuable. It makes you learn, or begin to learn, to know your own body inside out. You're tuned so that if something is going wrong you know long before anybody else picks it up, and also it relates to whatever it is you're doing with your character, so the physical and mental business go hand in hand. You have to stay fit, and you learn how you can communicate a lot without words. All the muscles do what you tell them to – you're never on stage with your body doing things you don't know about or letting you down in terms of your concentration and your sustaining the character. You spend many hours each week just learning where to put tension, for whatever reason; where to relax; how to get yourself into a certain position and stay there. In other words, you're so programmed (because you know your instrument so well) that you slip in a card that says for this character I require so, so, so and so, and it stays there and you don't have to worry about dropping character, whether it's a limp or a twitch or a particular way of walking or standing or sitting or even a particular pitch to the voice. All that, you have under control. It's like while on stage performing I'm also standing in the wings – I don't know how else to put it – and I can gauge, I can feel (if I'm concentrating properly) what is happening with the audience as well as what's happening with my fellow players on stage. If the audience is straying or somebody is missing things or moves are wrong, you can bend, manipulate yourself, change the other actor, gauge the audience, get them back or make them laugh or cry or scream or whatever. You're there and you're aware. In some roles it's more pronounced; in others I don't watch myself so much. But the Laban theory says that the person left on stage is the total character.

It's easy to harmonize Laban theory with Stanislavski's method acting. I've taken from each the things that I could make my own, and now they've come together as perhaps me. I've stuck to the things that from that time I found to work — the memory exercises that perhaps define an aspect of a character. Over the years some of what I learnt has been finetuned to the point where I don't even remember that I do it. It's like breathing or walking.

Method acting can be dangerous. There was one actor who, if he had a role to play, would go out and live like the character for a spell. But once he wasn't able to come out of the role. I think the character was a street person and he went and spent an awful lot of time with winos and by the time he had finished playing the character he could no longer find where the character left off and he himself began.

I've had moments when I've been frightened silly. I'm thinking, *Christ, can I come down, or am I going to take all this home and not be able to get rid of it?* But in fact once you can stay out there and watch yourself play the character it won't happen.

Stanislavski works from the inside and demands that you use everything that happens to you. If something hurts you, once you've gotten over it you sit down, review it and file it so that, if you need it, it is there. If something wonderful happens to you, you remember not just the feeling of something wonderful happening but exactly how you reacted, what you felt and what you did.

I've found it has worked not only for the stage but for my own personal life as well, in that things happen and instead of being totally devastated — though there's a natural period of feeling a little sorry for yourself ("Poor me, why did it happen to me?"), but maybe over the years that period has gotten shorter and shorter — you review the experience, saying, "Now why did it happen? How did it happen, and how did I feel, how did I react?", and you file it away. I find that, maybe because of that approach, I end up not nearly as bitter as I could have been.

I think that because I had lived a little bit before I started my training I was able to get quite a lot more out of the sessions with the methods tutor than a lot of other students in the class. I didn't mind contributing some of the things that had happened to me — good, bad or indifferent — and this helped my development as a person as well as a performer. You get used to being exposed. Some of the characters I play make me feel like that. I find now that I hardly think of myself as having secrets, though there are certain things I don't particularly want to share.

Nell Carter, the lady who worked with us on Shakespeare, had been one of England's most famous Juliets. She gave me my first little boost when, about halfway through the term, she said, clearly indicating me, "Well at least there's one person in the class who speaks Shakespeare like a real person, instead of declaiming and posturing." That didn't make me a favourite with the class, but it meant I got an awful lot from Nell Carter. Another tutor was Valerie Hanson, who had been a fabulous actress and a great beauty. In an accident on her way to a performance her face got badly messed up and she was terribly bitter about this. But if she recognized potential she would give you special attention — for instance, she made me straighten my back. I had been unaware that I had a sort of curve and was slumping, until she said, "No, no, no, no, that will never do! Come on, I expect better from you!" There were a couple of other caring tutors who said, "You're here because you have talent. Be positive."

I am an intuitive performer, some tutors told me, and therefore vulnerable when working with actors who are extremely technical. I depend on the other actors to give, so that together we create the circle of energy that makes the audience feel they're eavesdropping. Some schools of English acting that are purely technical can be off-putting because these actors avoid eye contact on stage, they tend to look or focus slightly off-right or off-left. It's like everything is worked out in the mind, with so many beats to that gesture, so many beats to that move. For the intuitive performer that style can be a big challenge, though it works very well in a farce.

We had several tutors in voice and speech. Clifford Turner, who wrote *Voice and Speech in the Theatre* which was the Bible for acting students, was a wonderful man, and frighteningly thorough. There was Audrey Ballard who dealt with phonetics and interpretation; and there was Dorothy Scott teaching phonetics and pronunciation. There was one other — she became my favourite, because I absolutely adored her voice and what she did with words. That was Catherine Fleming. She encouraged us to stand up straight and free the lungs. She was patient and worked very hard to help us get rid of kinks. You had to learn to relax and open your throat to speak, making the sound warm and round. To this day I hold on to and practise her exercises.

There were some negatives in my experience of RADA. When I got there I was afraid of speaking, because I sounded so different from the other students. Some tutors seem to think that if you're black and from the Caribbean or any black country, you won't be able to communicate in English. Also, their theatrical history was so vast and so well set that one easily felt like an outsider. There were things I wasn't sure I could handle, because I didn't understand them, I hadn't been exposed to them. Sometimes I thought, *What's the point of learning that? When I go home I'm never going to be asked to do that.* And although I was diligently studying all this wonderful standard English, these English customs and social graces and so on, nearly every time I got a role they wanted me to be from Trinidad, Jamaica or Nassau or South America.

Robin Midgely was the exception to that. I had worked with him in Jamaica. Now back in the UK, he was directing a television series, *Dixon of Dock Green*, and he gave me a role where it didn't matter whether I was black or not, and in which I spoke standard English. Because of him, I worked with the extraordinarily talented actor Judi Dench.

I sometimes worried about losing myself; a black girl, a black woman, a black performer, with no intention whatever of staying over there. But a few tutors and wellwishers said,

"Look, you're going to go home, What you should do is take the best of what is offered here, make it your own, learn as much as you can, so that you can make good use of it, but don't ever let anyone change who you are. Keep your own accent, keep your Jamaican identity, and become a rounded performer." That was excellent advice. It paid off. I learnt to do several non-Jamaican voices — including Indian, Bajan, Trinidadian and Cockney. Later, when I went to Australia, I played a number of English characters.

When we tackled the business of improvisations, what startled me and interested me greatly — I still use it from time to time — was imitating the body language of animals. I recall being in a production directed by Lloyd Reckord years later in Jamaica — I think it was *The Rose Slip* — and one of the ladies had a bit of a problem with understanding her character. Lloyd said, "You know a duck?" And she said yes. Then Lloyd said, "When the duck walk? Show me!" She was at sea. Lloyd said, "Go home go study it and come back." When she came back and did the walk, it was perfect for her character. I remembered what I had learnt in the methods classes.

Training in movement wasn't just about moving well as a person, it was also learning period movement — how you walk when you're wearing period clothes, gown, or elaborate, sometimes restraining, costumes. And if you have period dances you would have to learn the style and patterns of the particular time. I won the V.C. Buckley Award for style and the wearing of costume.

We were also taught mime — by the same Miss Phillips and her assistant who had taught Miss Lou. They remembered Miss Lou. Miss Phillips actually asked if I knew Louise Bennett, and I said, "Yes, ma'am, I do."

Fencing was part of the curriculum. It was felt that it would help with posture and would prove handy in various productions, including some Shakespeare plays. We were very fortunate: our Polish instructor had been an Olympic fencer. The training proved valuable when I played Annie in the LTM's *Pirate Princess*. I could handle the sword.

I had some physical problems. I have a curvature in my spine that gives me backache, but the school always arranged for any kind of therapy one needed. I had passed out during one of the rigorous movement classes and they sent me to the physiotherapist, who happened to be blind. He explained it all — the curvature — and said perhaps I might not be able to do ballet and do full extensions (which I already knew). He gave me exercises that helped me move well. The school paid for all of that, as well as for treatment when I tore ligaments in my ankle during a performance.

One of the negative things at drama school was the bitchiness of students who resented me and the opportunities that came my way. During term breaks — holidays — I always had a paying job in the office as an assistant to the school secretary. This was a blessing and a great financial help. Also, the principal knew it was difficult for black performers to get really decent roles, so if something came up — if he knew of it — he'd send me up for it. I would get time off to do it but had to keep up with my classwork and assignments. Some of the students were terribly catty about what they saw as special treatment.

To get a little experience, we were allowed to work in a number of professional productions. For instance, the tutor would select you and you would go off to the Royal Shakespeare Company and be a member of the chorus.

Every year there was a Shakespeare Festival at the Southwark Cathedral, and each year they chose two students from each drama school. I got chosen to represent RADA in 1962. I was absolutely terrified. But, as it happened, an experienced English actor took me under his wing, and every lunch time he'd call out, "Leonie, where are you? Come along, young Forbes." And we would go through the piece that had been selected. So I gave a good account of myself at the festival, and the principal, John Ferland, was pleased.

Some of my fellow students became famous – people such as John Hurt, Ian McShane, David Warner. The one I knew best was David Warner, a nice person who was very helpful. When I came in he was just beginning his final year, and he would talk with us, the new students, and give us pointers.

Acting is pretty desperate work, because there are at least two hundred other very capable, talented people lining up for every part. When I was graduating most of the parts for blacks were as extras. But it was hard for English actors too, because much of the work available was in television, for which employers tended to choose performers not so much on talent as on whether they looked the part. You could do it with your eyes closed, and you still wouldn't get the part. As students we worked out a list of things to do while "resting" — like addressing envelopes, or washing dishes, or driving a cab, or anything.

No one wanted to be there at graduation to receive the diploma. What everybody hoped for was that when they called your name, someone would explain your absence — "Filming!" or "In such-and-such a production." When my graduation came in mid-1963, I was filming in Manchester.

Cinderella

In the United Kingdom, age 22

Chapter Five

Love and Marriage

My first husband, "Bunny", I met through a friend in 1957. I was working in the Radio Education Unit at Mona and rehearsing for the pantomime *Busha Bluebeard*. My friend came by to watch rehearsals and I was introduced. Bunny was a civil servant, four or so years older than I. He was quiet, well spoken, tall and attractive. I thought him rather nice, and he seemed focused on me. We dated for about a year and I thought it was love because I wanted him near me all the time.

In 1958 I went off to Trinidad with the pantomime to the West Indies Festival of Arts. He telephoned to say how much he missed me. In those days an overseas call was really something. I took it to mean that love was in the air. He proposed in August. "Would you mind waiting until next year to get married and we'll get engaged at Christmas?" he said. When Christmas came, I got a beautiful gold bracelet but no engagement ring. He explained that he had given the money to his mother. I was disappointed and upset and a bit worried how Aunt G and Uncle Weddie, who were expecting the event, would react. In fact, they quarrelled with me.

Bunny and I also quarrelled. Making up afterwards we got somewhat carried away, and although we came to our senses quickly the horse had gone through the gate. A few weeks later I began feeling funny and the doctor confirmed that I was pregnant. When I called Bunny he surprised me. He couldn't understand how that could be. He was unprepared, as socially vulnerable as I was, and love seemed to take some backward steps immediately. I was forced to collect myself and begin preparations for my new status and responsibilities.

The next few months were fraught with problems, not least of which was Bunny's unexplained absence. Getting to and from my job was a challenge, especially as one of the complications of the pregnancy was passing out anywhere, anytime. I was warned by my obstetrician not to be alone. Truth be told, I don't know how I would have survived that period of my life without the caring and practical support of a friend and co-worker, Alma Mock Yen (she was Alma Hylton then). In addition to my mental and physical stress there was the huge issue of Aunt G and Uncle Weddie who knew nothing of my condition. I was at a complete loss how to tell them, especially how to explain why there was no husband to introduce.

At the beginning of my fifth month my boss, Hugh Morrison, who had been extremely supportive, offered to help. He would arrange my transfer to WIBS in Grenada.

There I could continue working in broadcasting and have my baby without any harmful gossip. I would be able to raise my child and make something of my life. I jumped at the chance and began preparations to travel.

A few days before my departure Bunny showed up, wanting to put things right. He said he would accompany me to my Aunt G and Uncle Weddie. After very careful consideration – despite my earlier resolve to go it alone – I accepted his offer. The meeting was traumatic. Suffice it to say a wedding was arranged, which actually took place a couple weeks later, on May 18, 1959. Not a marriage of love as I saw it, not the one I had dreamt of earlier. It was simply to save face.

After the wedding, any notion of love receded further and further away from my heart because, after honeymoon night, Bunny remained an absentee until the morning my labour pains began. I called him to let him know that the doctor had instructed me to go to the hospital right away and that I was waiting for him to transport me. I waited and waited and waited, to no avail. Finally, pain-wracked and fearful, I had to accept my landlady's offer to drive me to the hospital. The following morning, September 15, 1959 at quarter past three, when they placed my son in my arms, I felt the joy and wonder of motherhood and knew that for my son's sake I would never give up but would carry on, regardless of Bunny.

For the next several months I soldiered on, with the kind and generous support of Aunt G and Uncle Weddie and of Bunny's father, Sam, as well as a few close friends.

My job as a JBC announcer complemented my work in theatre, and being on air helped boost my self-esteem. Almost overnight I was somebody. I was being talked about, written about in the newspapers and recognized as a promising talent. Suddenly, in the wake of my new achievements, I became someone worthy of acknowledgement as the mother of Bunny's son, and his parents put pressure on him to take up his rightful position as husband and father.

To give him his due, he tried; but at this point, after all that had passed, I was indifferent. The late and lukewarm attempt to capture what never really was, and to actually live in the same space for three months or so, did not work. I didn't even want to try. I had grown accustomed to facing the music alone; so, without hesitation, we decided to go our separate ways.

By the time I met Carlos, months later, the old hurts had subsided. I continued my work at the JBC, including outside broadcasts at the Carib Cinema where Top 10 Hit Parade shows were presented each week. The JBC Orchestra was in charge, with greats like Sonny Bradshaw, Bertie King, Baba Motta, as well as Carlos who not only played several instruments but also wrote and arranged for the orchestra.

I was ready to discover and explore the possibilities of being in love again. Almost as if planned, Carlos's friendship and support seemed timely. He was a talented musician and greatly admired as such. Some people thought him a bit eccentric but to me he was just an individualist. His wide knowledge, his stimulating conversation, his perspective on life, his seemingly casual approach to mundane things, and his deep appreciation for the simple joys of life caught and held my attention. I felt that we knew and respected each other, and that the pluses outweighed the minuses. We became good friends.

Life was moving along nicely. Aunt G and Uncle Weddie were back in town and, most important, I was together with my son, Robert, the centre of my young world. We were all together.

Trouble don't set like rain. Out of the blue my sixteen-month-old son became ill. What appeared to be just an ordinary flu attack turned out to be an acute attack of nephritis, a kidney problem, with accompanying complications. He was retaining fluid. He was swelling up. Shock, disbelief, fear, agonizing concern tore me apart. Many sleepless nights, no appetite. I could barely concentrate on my broadcasting shift. I turned to cigarettes and coffee to keep me going.

Close on the heels of learning that my son would probably never become a teenager, came the news of a glorious, totally unexpected opportunity — a scholarship to the RADA in London. What was I going to do? In his offhand yet forceful manner, Carlos intervened, or maybe I should say took charge. I was doing, I thought, a reasonable job of holding myself together and pressing forward. He wasn't fooled. He had been listening to my on air presentations and he wasn't fooled.

He called me: "What time you finish work today?"

"My shift ends in about half an hour, why?"

"I'll be waiting downstairs for you."

And he was. Our first stop was Medical Associates where Robert had been admitted. (The institution's first crib was bought for him.) During the ride to the hospital Carlos got the full story out of me. He took me for a meal and insisted that I eat; then he drove me to Bohemia — a jazz club off the Molynes Road — and told me, "Sit." He opened the piano and played and played and played, beautiful music, familiar and unfamiliar.

After having played music for a good while, he came to sit beside me. In his characteristically dispassionate voice, he said: "People say I'm cold and hard and I guess you think me tough and all that, but when I lost my twin brother suddenly I thought I would never love anybody again. Thing is, you have to carry on. I suppose you have to cry and all that, so go ahead and get it out of your system. You certainly don't want people to see you in this state. You don't want pity, do you? So your little boy is sick. You're not the first woman to have a sick child and you have a job to do." Then he moved back to the piano and kept playing. The tears poured and poured until I was completely wrung out, for which I thanked Carlos, but I still couldn't decide whether to leave Robert and go to London. Carlos had an answer for that too. He said, "Your staying here won't make the baby better and your going won't kill him. Opportunities like this come once in a lifetime. So get out of here. You'll be fine. Go do your stuff 'cause I know you have it in you."

The rest happened in a rush like a machine on fast-forward. Aunt G promised to take good care of Robert, and she did just that for five years. London was on.

When I was leaving for London in 1961, Carlos asked me to find a young lady there with twins he had fathered. She had not kept in touch, and he wanted me to find her and let him know if she needed anything. That was the moment I realized we were not meant to be anything more than good friends. I agreed to honour his request. We stayed in touch. Distance did not weaken our bond of friendship and he followed my career throughout the years.

London was a vast new world. The city was cold, lonely and alien — different from anywhere I'd ever been or known. I had a little attic room with a mattress on the floor and the company of my landlady Jill and her small son, Justin. But fortunately for me there were a few friends who had gone to London ahead of me — Charlie Hyatt, Vernon Estick, Karl Binger, Franklyn Cousins and Trevor Rhone. I wasted no time in making contact.

RADA was somewhat intimidating at first, yet truly exciting, and I was making great strides by the end of my first term when Charlie and Vernon invited me to travel with them to see Karl in a production. Knowing what a fun-loving crowd that was, I didn't hesitate to take the long train trip. It turned out to be a great evening. To my surprise, a handsome young man named Keith joined the group as we settled in at the pub for the customary after-the-show catching up and "giving laugh fi peas soup". Keith was studying to be a vet on a scholarship from Jamaica and it turned out that his hall of residence was within walking distance of RADA. When the evening ended we had each other's telephone numbers and mailing addresses.

I was flattered and touched when he called within a few days and came by to visit. I had no hesitation at all when he invited me out. He was tall enough, good-looking, bright, well mannered and well put together. I had known him slightly in Jamaica, having seen him perform in a couple of pantomimes, as well as in some of Orford St John's productions.

It was easy to get involved in activities at the West Indian Student Centre Union, and Keith and I soon found ourselves with a folk group there. We designed costumes, choreographed and danced as well. The group went to folk dance festivals in Ireland, worked with a limbo group that visited Germany, Belgium and France, and travelled later to a youth rally in Helsinki, where we actually met the first Russian astronaut, Gagarin. Keith and I were constantly together. By August 1962 I realized there was a strong attachment that was reciprocated, in spite of my reservations about this "falling in love" condition.

Keith was very much around for my graduation, mid-1963,

and to my surprise he told me, "If you leave here you're going to marry someone else, so you'd better hang out here because I want to marry you." I was still legally married, but as soon as my divorce from Bunny became final, Keith came by with a beautiful engagement ring, and we were married soon after my graduation from RADA.

Keith was doing extremely well at university and I was working on BBC TV and Radio and on Independent Television (ITV). In January of '64 I realized I was pregnant. Keith was elated. Although the pregnancy had its complications, delivery was natural and speedy. I had the thrill of watching my daughter Karen come into the world. Her father was over-joyed.

The next six months were challenging for Keith, Karen and me, but Charlie Hyatt and his wife Vera were tremendously helpful. Seven months after Karen's arrival I realized I had "gone up the hill" again. In December 1965 our son Moyo came into the world – by C-section. Keith was as proud as a peacock of his healthy, beautiful baby son. After that we had just a month to pack up and return to Jamaica. It was no simple task taking care of two babies and packing to go home, but Keith had graduated at the end of 1965 and we had to be on our way. We returned to Jamaica early in 1966.

I was eager to get home to see my first son Robert, meet my new in-laws, and get together with my own family and friends and the theatre fraternity. I was also keen to impart what I'd learnt, having completed my RADA training with distinction. But most of all I wanted to set up home for my husband and children. Within a few months I was back on staff at the JBC. Keith landed a job with the Ministry of Agriculture and was off and running except that he was based in Hanover. He could only be home on weekends — which put a bit of a strain on the marriage, but we worked through it.

Chapter Six

Continuing in Radio

W hile at RADA I got involved with the BBC Repertory Theatre Company which sent material to Africa and the Caribbean. There were the *Calling the Caribbean* programmes, and programmes that dealt with letters from listeners all over the world. I also got involved with schools broadcasting with the BBC.

After I graduated from RADA and got married to Keith, there was a schools broadcasting series in which I played a little boy called Martin from Jamaica, with Jeremy Verity as the teacher. One day the executive producer came in to meet the little boy that he was quite taken with. The director giggled and said, "Martin, would you come round and meet the producer." The executive producer nearly died when he saw me – a woman, five-going-six months pregnant. The series went well. It was released on LPs and was distributed to the West Indies and other places. Under the guidance of Newton James (who later joined the JBC) I also did some work with the Nuffield Foundation – mostly television for Third World countries – health science, how to deliver a baby in the bush, to speak English, a little geography, a little everything. I enjoyed every minute of it.

When I returned to Jamaica in 1966 it was as though I had never left, because news of what I had been doing in England had filtered back. Audrey Chong, who was with the Jamaica Information Service (JIS) at the time, interviewed me on television and asked me to do various accents. Right after that I was invited by Harvey Ennevor, who was then general manager at JBC, to rejoin the station. So I went straight back into radio.

I got a slot to do a programme called *Jamaica Woman*: I introduced poetry and short stories, and got the themes composed and performed by Ernie Ranglin because I thought it was high time we went Jamaican. I was with that programme for nearly a year, then Beverley Anderson joined and we both worked on it. We organized a group of women who would meet for coffee and cookies every Saturday morning. We took stacks of tapes, lots of batteries, put the tape recorder in the centre of the table, threw out questions and comments and listened to the ladies respond. We would edit the tapes during the weekend and then, each morning that week, play five-minute segments of what the women had said – no water, no light, children suffering, pigs and goats running all over the place, and so on.

Somebody from the prime minister's office phoned and said Mr Shearer wanted to talk with Beverley and me. He thought we might have set the women up to say these things, which we denied. At our suggestion, he invited the women to Jamaica House one Saturday morning and allowed us to tape the session there. As a result, people got stand-pipes and electricity where they didn't have them before, and we got things for the children. Operation Friendship, with Annabella Ogden and Rev. Webster Edwards, started about that time, and we helped to get it off the ground. We begged for food, bedding, material, equipment. We encouraged people to go and meet the children and play with them. We took some of the children on sponsored field trips, for example, to visit the School for the Deaf in Brown's Town. It was exciting radio. Eventually there was a television version of the same programme, with a broader cross-section of women – including some of the ladies from upper St Andrew who had a little more money and a lot more time to come in and talk, and they sometimes donated yards and yards of material. People would offer what they could. A little lady might make coconut drops and sell them and give the money to buy bits of cloth to make undergarments for the children or nighties. The paint companies would contribute paint. The whole community was involved.

I worked at JBC until 1968 when I left for Australia with Keith. He had won a Commonwealth Scholarship to do postgraduate work in veterinary medicine, and he refused to go without me. Flattering as that was, and proud as I was of his achievement, I was concerned about having to leave my children. Aunt G came to the rescue again, taking all three under her wing with full support from Keith's parents.

Chapter Seven

Australia

As soon as we arrived in Brisbane — even while we were still looking for a flat — Mrs Moody, the wife of Keith's supervisor, let the papers loose on me. People came and interviewed me. There was a whole page on all the theatre training I had had, and the roles I had done, and I got invited to auditions for *The Merchant of Venice*.

Merrick Needham, my former general manager at JBC, had given me a letter to the Australian Broadcasting Corporation (ABC). When I finally saw the ABC gentleman he said, "Darling, the only job I could offer you is my own, and I'm sorry, I really need it, you know."

I registered with a typing pool, because I liked to type and I thought I could earn some pennies there. My first job was in the news department of one of the television stations. I did so well they didn't want me to leave. But I said, "Look, I'm not a newsroom person." Next thing I know, a lady phoned me to ask if I would join in a TV game show.

I didn't have to go banging on many doors. A series of lucky accidents and there we were! I was assigned to the IBM typing pool for a week, and halfway through the week they were so pleased — they probably didn't expect black people to have any sense — that the gentleman asked me to do one of those IQ tests, and apparently I did well. Then he said, "The librarian is going off. Would you like to work in this department?" I said, "I don't know a thing about it." He said, "You can learn. According to your IQ, you can learn." And there I was. I stayed in that job for the rest of my time in Australia. They'd give me time off to go and perform, traipse all over Australia, because they figured the publicity they got made it a good idea — newspaper articles would identify me as performing by courtesy of IBM.

Working at IBM was an experience. I had absolutely no training in librarianship, but I put my mind to it. I went off to Sydney to seminars and things. When IBM were building new headquarters in Brisbane I helped design the library for them. They solicited my ideas and implemented them.

I think I changed the lifestyle down there a little bit, at least the lifestyle of the people who worked at IBM. There was noticeable gender division, women one way and men another — you'd find that in the lunch room the men went over to one side. I said, "Come on, let's get together. Where did you go yesterday? How's your wife? How are the children? What do you like to do?" We got invited to rugby matches and family picnics, to go hiking, to go sailing. I don't like water, but I actually spent some time on Stradbroke Island, a holiday place off the Brisbane coast. I had to close my eyes tight to cross in the motor boat, but once I was on land again I was all right.

I did a lot of theatre. I started out with the College Players (who later became the Queensland Theatre Company). I did some Shakespeare with them, and I acted in *The Owl and the Pussycat* opposite Keith. They thought using two black performers would stimulate interest, and it did – we had a packed house every night. I worked with La Boîte Theatre Company to start a Sunday series of activities – words, movement, music – in which nearly everybody who was interested could take part. The series was very popular. I did some radio plays – the gentleman in charge of the ABC Department of Drama was also RADA-trained and he welcomed me. I had my hands full – different characters, including English characters, Amerindian characters, Māori characters, all sorts of roles.

I also did a lot of work for ABC's School on Air programmes, which sometimes meant writing a script to tell them a little about Jamaica or the Caribbean or whatever. Some of the children in Australia are schooled by radio because they live hundreds of miles from their nearest neighbours. I also got asked to help at a high school where I was given a bunch of problem children – they were bright but they wouldn't settle down, and their marks were terrible. It was hoped that through drama I might steady them, improve their grades immeasurably. I made them do everything, including write the script and make the set and the costumes. The principal

was so pleased that about six months later I was asked to
do a paper to present to the Ministry of Education about the
use of drama in schools. I haven't studied drama in education.
I was just going by what I felt and the needs I could see.

Australians have their own folk stories — mostly legends
based on aboriginal characters — and they gave me a book
called *Children of the Dark* which had a number of tales. I
developed a script from that. I worked with a fabulous
young music student from Queensland University and we
produced a musical.

I had a radio programme on Saturday nights at nine o'clock,
built around Caribbean music, all the different kinds of
Caribbean music. I sent home for books so I could do research
and say a little about Caribbean history and culture.
That programme ran for almost the whole two years I
was in Australia. It even went out as far as New Guinea,
as I discovered when I stopped there on the way home
to Jamaica.

In Christmas 1969 I did a number of five-minute fillers
for television, dressed up in fancy clothes and singing
Christmas carols, with Geoffrey Rush playing the guitar —
the Geoffrey Rush who later won an Oscar for his work in
Shine. By the time I was ready to leave Australia I couldn't
walk on the street without being recognized —"Oh, we enjoyed
it so much, I hope you're going to stay with us another
year." I said, "Thank you, but sorry. I have to go home."

The involvement in theatre was tremendous. I think the
biggest thing that came of out it was the production of *The
Merchant of Venice* which was an exam set book for a couple of

years. I waited about three months after auditioning for the role of Portia, and then I was told, "Look, we haven't found anybody as good and you have everything we want. It's just that you're black. We're going to go with you, and the publicity will work for us."

When the production was going to Canberra, some of the people went three weeks ahead of the rest of the company and they didn't get one word of publicity, but the afternoon I arrived "yuh ears couldn eat grass" (as my grandmother would say) — radio interviews one after the other, TV interviews, and the newspaper people were there. I guess my blackness caught their fancy, and they were impressed by the fact that I was trained at an English institution. It was a little frightening, because I had to do well; but I did, at least in Canberra — the review was headlined "Rich Merchant" and I got very nice comments. About six or seven months later when their national company, the Australian Ensemble, did *Merchant of Venice* in the same theatre, the headline was "A Thin Merchant", and the paragraph that will never leave my memory said that their production lacked the perfection of the College Players' Portia.

Our production was filmed and was used in schools to show how to make Shakespeare real. The kids loved it. We even performed in a boxing ring at one stage of the game, so that more of the children out in the bush could see the production. My Portia was probably the best of the classic roles I've played. I was made up to look more Spanish than Negro, like I had a nice tan, and I had red hair. The Prince of Morocco was an Australian white man made up to look black.

Towards the end of the run of *Merchant* with the College Players, the director (Bryan Nason) mentioned that the Queensland National Company was about to be formed and he wanted something grand and spectacular for the inaugural production. He had thought of doing *The Royal Hunt of the Sun* but he didn't think he could get Australian performers to appear like Amerindians. He said, "They're an outdoor, sporty people, but they're awkward. All that sensual movement, they can't do it." I said, "Of course they can." I didn't think I'd ever hear anything more. Then, about three months after the last performance of *Merchant,* he called me up. "Remember you said you could turn Australians into Indians? Well, you're on. We're going to do *The Royal Hunt of the Sun* and the job is yours. Thirty to thirty-five young Australians from Brisbane." I thought, *Dear God, what have I done?*

I took the university library apart and went to every bookshop and read everything I could find on the Aztecs. Then we started rehearsals. Weeks before they even saw the text, we did movement sessions and I had to try to remember everything that Ivy Baxter taught me and that I had seen Rex Nettleford do, getting the pelvic girdle free. After about three weeks, when I thought they were feeling and looking different, Bryan did a fantastic thing. He got an old church to rehearse in, full of atmosphere and strange spirits, and he called me one afternoon and said, "For rehearsals tonight, after you've done your movement thing, I want you to trust me and leave them to me for a while. I don't want you to leave, but I don't want you to say anything. Whatever happens, don't be surprised, don't be shocked, don't react."

When I got to the rehearsal space I realized that there were lights set up around this empty stone floor, no benches or anything, and some mats for the actors to work on. After they had gone through the movement exercises and were nicely warmed up, Bryan put out the lights and then the spotlights came on, a reddish glow through which we could only vaguely make out actors lying on the mats. He started talking about the Aztecs, how they lived, what motivated them. "And of course," he said, "they weren't encumbered by clothes, they had that kind of freedom..." In about fifteen minutes every single person on those mats had taken off everything. Then he said, "Now get up, and begin to move." It was incredible to see: all those self-conscious people I'd been working with for weeks, they were transformed. Then Bryan killed the lights and said, "Now you can get dressed." He found me and said, "Let's go outside and leave them." Not a sound. Nobody spoke. Not a word.

When the play opened there was a burst of applause from the audience — and not because of the wigs and the body make-up. They were seeing Amerindians.

The Merchant of Venice

The Merchant of Venice

Chapter Eight

Divorce and Marriage

In Brisbane, wonderful opportunities to do theatre came my way, stimulating my growth and development in that field. Keith likewise continued to excel, and as a couple we were gaining recognition for our talents and creative efforts. However, success invites special attention, and I was forced to acknowledge possible threats. Dealing with that emotional pressure magnified the separation from my children. I remember sending cards, letters and little gifts regularly as I couldn't hear their voices – telephoning was not then easily possible. Later on I learnt that Aunt G had put away everything and waited for a special occasion which never seemed to come – a peculiar habit of her generation. Some things survived until our return in 1970.

I will never forget the first meeting with the children, something I'd been looking forward to and dreaming about, the moment when they would fly into my arms and we'd hug and dance with joy and happiness. It never happened. I remember standing there with my arms wide open, grinning from ear to ear as they stood frozen, uncertain, looking to Aunt G for permission to greet me.

I was so torn up that I vowed then and there that I would not, under any circumstances whatever, leave them again. I wanted to run off with them right away, but it took a couple of weeks to establish a home and be together as a family. Within a couple of months I realized I was "up the hill" again — with our third child. By this time, Keith was consumed with his career and achievements to the point where he barely had time to deal with much more than the basic requirements of a husband and father.

Struggling to take care of family while trying to hold on to my job was taxing, to say the least; the pregnancy wasn't easy either. Dianne was born on January 27, 1971 — a C-section saved us both — and there was general joy. So once again, despite all odds, I came through it all. Life was back to normal, as normal as could be expected with Keith still busy and caught up in his career; me trying my utmost to run my home and press on with my job and theatre interests.

It seemed that the distance between us might widen and lead to the breakdown of family life and even the marriage itself. I prayed it would not be so, but ultimately I had to face the fact that we were growing apart. The marriage was no longer working.

Funny thing about important dates in that period of my existence. My birthday is June 14, his October 14. We got married on July 27; Karen was born September 27, Moyo on December 27, and Dianne on January 27. With a tie-up like that I thought our lives together would be magical, but they were not.

As Keith grew older and more established in the society, he had become a typical Jamaican macho-man. I decided to give him the space he obviously needed to show off his prowess. Quietly I began to plan how to move on with my children and continue to enjoy the successes of my own career. I needed to enjoy that feeling of worth engendered by what I had achieved so far, both as a mother and a public figure.

I sought professional advice and concluded that court proceedings would have a devastating effect on the children. It seemed best to leave them where they were with Keith, take the time to settle into my own space, arrange to spend quality time with them and work towards their eventually joining me. This was the single most difficult decision I had to make, apart from the time many years earlier when I took up the scholarship to RADA, leaving Robert with Aunt G.

Within a couple of years – in 1974 – my second divorce was final. I did manage to spend quality time with my children; made sure they knew they were loved and had my full support. With time they adjusted to the arrangement. My career meanwhile kept growing to new heights and I could appreciate fully my new status. In the twinkling of an eye the children were grown. One by one and completely of their own volition they chose to be with me.

My third marriage was to Gary. I had seen him performing in a pantomime and thought he was talented, energetic, with lots of presence, then promptly forgot about him. Several months later I agreed to do the title role in Brecht's *Mother Courage* with director Norman Rae. The young man was at the auditions and ended up getting the role of one of my sons. He missed a few rehearsals and I decided it was time for our professional pep talk.

"You can't build a character and its relevant relationships if you're absent. You must come to rehearsals on time or inform someone when you can't." He said he had the flu. I brushed his reply aside as a lame excuse until I felt his forehead; he was burning up. I was a little ashamed of my insistence. Soon after that, I learnt that he lived a good distance away — in the hills — and getting to and from rehearsals, especially late at night, was difficult and dangerous. My guilt kicked in and I offered him accommodation until opening night. In that way he could focus on his performance, which I knew would contribute greatly to the success of the production, and at the same time give me a chance to know him, establish a comfort level as is my custom when a character interacts directly with the one I am playing.

During his stay at my house, he adapted as if he were a relative. He got on very well with my children, so much so that when the production ended he continued to visit. I too began to enjoy his company and look forward to his visits. Without conscious effort or planning he seemed to become part of my family and was around us all the time. Without any warning we arrived at a stage where he was reluctant to leave and I equally, if unwisely, wanted him to stay. I thought to myself, What the dickens is this? I would have to think very carefully. The differences in our ages that never mattered before suddenly became in my mind a huge factor, not just because of society's expectations but out of concern for my children.

I had been somewhat lonely, but that sounded like a lame excuse even to me. Gary was engaging, caring, friendly and warm, and made me laugh at myself. We did simple things together which brought me a level of inner calm that I'd long forgotten. There was a kind of harmony about me and my home that I had longed for and ignored not having. Now happiness was closing in on me and I could not shrug it off. I liked how I felt and who I was when he was around. I felt normal, natural, feminine, happy and cared for, and most of all, important to him, someone other than my children. I didn't know whether this was or could be love, or just a crazy phase. Whatever it was it felt right. Young or otherwise, he was the person who helped me reach this comfort level within myself, a feeling that had evaded me for the longest time.

I knew he had a baby son, Ishmael. He brought him around a few times. This made no difference. He and his baby were welcome to join the family. When he asked me to marry him I said yes, and we were married in December 1978. Gary wanted his son to be with us, but there was resistance from Ishmael's mother who started making unreasonable demands and was supported fully by Gary's mother who did not approve of our relationship. For a while these factors created pressure and tension, but they soon passed. Gary was grateful and proud that I had stood with him throughout and I felt a contentment I had not known since the first heady years of my marriage to Keith.

We had wonderful times together, Gary and I. We explored Jamaica and travelled – as far away as Morocco. Still I kept reminding myself that he was so much younger than I and searching to find himself in terms of a career and direction.

I saw him through many changes, the most significant of which was his newfound culture – Rastafari. I did not oppose him nor was I put off by it, as it was part and parcel of a way of life I'd come to know and appreciate. I never imagined that things would reach such intensity that he would want to take the message far and wide through music and the establishment of communes.

I remember smiling to myself and thinking, *All good things must come to an end*, and accepting that I had come to the end of our road together, and that I could no longer be a part of his dream. I let him go. I assured him of my continued support, wished him all the very best, and waved him goodbye in 1985.

As always I pressed on; putting new energy into my career and enjoying my grown children without feeling any sense of loss as with my previous liaisons.

Glowing with her fourth child

With Dianne, Moyo and Karen, 1974

Chapter Nine

Dreams and Visions

*W*hen I was about seven years old I lived with Aunt G and her sister Aunt Florence in a rented house at the top of Church Street. It was a huge property with a two-storey mansion, and most evenings, especially on weekends, you would hear beautiful music being played or sung there. Two doors away there was a Lodge meeting-place which used to terrify me: you could hear chains and chanting and all sorts of things.

One evening – during a period when the family was plagued with illnesses of one sort or another, we just couldn't keep good health – I was playing on the verandah of the old house, and when I looked up at the wall on the southern side of the yard I saw a lady in a long dress and wearing a large broad hat and she was pointing towards the step at the side of the house. I felt really weird so I ran inside. Aunt Florence said, "What's wrong with you? Why you don't stop running up and down the place? It's getting dark and you might fall down." I said, "A lady out there!" "Which lady?" "She's over by the wall against the mango tree." Aunt Florence came out to see and said, "Nobody out here! What she look like?" "I don't know what she look like 'cause she turn sideways." "What she doing?" I told my aunt the lady was pointing at the side.

I heard my Aunt Florence and Aunt G muttering together. A few days later I heard Aunt Florence say she would be going to the country early the next day and would be back in the afternoon. She went to St Thomas, and a couple of nights after her return they dug up the ground at the foot of the steps, found a jar and a small thread-bag with stuff in it and some coins. Following specific instructions they disposed of all the stuff.

Two or three nights later I was awakened by a strange sound and, peeking through the window, I saw the little old woman who lived in a room at the back of the yard walking towards the gate with a sheet of zinc on her head with bundles on it. No one ever saw her again.

From Church Street we moved to our own house at the top of King Street where a couple of things happened. Aunt G had a friend, Doris Johnson, who was a teacher in Trinityville, St Thomas. Whenever Miss Johnson came to Kingston I'd have to vacate my bed and sleep on a folding cot set up in the dining room between the table and the wall. For a few nights on one of these visits I would come awake, hear footsteps come from the living room into the dining room, walk by the safe, around the dining table, pass my bed and go back out through the living room. I always felt very strange but said nothing to anyone.

One night the footsteps came in, went around by the safe, and stopped as if searching for something. By the time the footsteps got to the side of my cot, I was cold as ice and covered with goose bumps but couldn't make a sound. I felt a hand poke me in my side and the footsteps departed. I screamed. Everybody came running in. "What's the matter, what happen?" "Somebody just come in here and jook me in my side." Aunt Florence as usual wanted details so I told the story. She said, "G, don't let the pickney sleep out here alone again, or put a light." For that night I slept in Aunt G's room but always had a light after that whenever I had to sleep in the dining room.

Shortly after that I returned from a Sunday School picnic just at twilight. I was sitting at the dining table eating when I looked up and saw a woman looking at me through the living room window. I shook my head, blinked rapidly, looked away, and when I looked back at the window the woman was still staring at me. I had that weird feeling again so I ran outside as fast as I could. Aunt G wanted to know why I'd left the rest of the dinner so I told her there was a lady looking at me through the window.

"Don't be stupid, nobody out there!" she said. But Aunt Florence wanted to know what she looked like. I told her. They looked at each other and Aunt G went to her room and got a box from underneath her bed, searched it and came up with a photograph. The person I had described was in that photograph and wearing the same dress. She was "Aunt Fanny", a courtesy aunt I never knew. She had died years before in childbirth and the baby, a little girl, was living with us. I never played rough or pushed her again.

A few years later I had another dream that has remained with me and is still as vivid as the night I dreamt it. Aunt G had gone to America and I was with my grandmother in the country for the period and was attending the Merrywood Elementary School which was in the same building where they held church services on Sundays. I dreamt I was playing marbles by myself in the school yard when a figure approached me; he was dressed in robes of brown and black and had long wavy hair and a moustache. He stretched out his hand and gave me a tin-can with a handle (a converted condensed milk tin) and said, "Take this and keep it; as long as you do you will never want." And he went off. Years later, thinking about it, I believe it was a kind of directive: humble myself and never forget my beginnings (tin-can as opposed to a china or enamel cup). Truth is, whenever I'm down and out or in difficulty, someone or something always turns up to help.

Sometimes I'd say things that turned out to be totally accurate — for instance, when I was leaving St George's Girls' School to go to the country and was asked by school friends what I was going to do in the country and I declared glibly that I was going to go to school, learn to play the piano and write sketches to perform. It turned out exactly like that. A directive came from Aunt G to send me to more piano lessons and at the end of my first term at school I wrote a skit about a South Parade peddler and dressed up in my grandmother's clothes and shoes. Head teacher Mr Campbell was very pleased and said, "Keep it up!"

Until I was fourteen or fifteen I had vivid dreams of family members and of flying everywhere. I dreamt of my Uncle Eric lying in hospital with the family gathered around him; he raised himself up, said something to Aunt G, lay back down and died. I told Aunt G about the dream and she ignored me. A few months later my uncle was very sick and went into hospital. Shortly after, I arrived home from school to find the house empty and strangely still. When Aunt G got home later that afternoon she told us that Uncle Eric had died exactly as I had described. She was quiet for a while, then told me quite firmly never to mention my dreams after that; I should keep them to myself. So I kept my dreams to myself although I continued to dream. Eventually they happened with less frequency and were not nearly as detailed.

When I first went to England, I was collected at the airport. The moment we turned on the road to the house where I was going to stay, I knew it. I knew every turn, everything. I walked straight to the door of my room. I knew exactly where I was going, and the house, the room, everything.

With my son Robert very ill when I left for RADA, I was told that everything that could be done was being done in Jamaica and that I should leave him where he was comfortable. I took his medical records to England, so we could try and get him to England if anything more could be done. One night, out of the blue, I shot out of bed, distressed and weeping and carrying on, and I couldn't understand why. Then a few weeks later I got a letter which told me that the baby had been very, very ill and wouldn't eat, just at the time I had felt distressed — so ill they didn't think he would last the night. Aunt G told me later that that particular night she had given up hope, everybody had given up hope, though she had written to Oral Roberts. She washed the child and put him to bed, and went to sleep herself, instead of sitting up. She thought, *He's either going to live or he's going to die*, and really she couldn't go any more. That was the night when, over in London, I jumped up in distress. Aunt G went to sleep, the Oral Roberts prayers happened, and when she got up in the morning my son was standing at the foot of the crib and saying, "I want porridge."

About three months before Bob Marley died in 1981, I had a vivid dream of a very large gathering, and the predominant thing was white and the Rastafarian colours and all these very ornately dressed people on the platform. When I woke up I told my husband, Gary, about it. I thought maybe he was going to take me to a Nyabinghi, and I forgot about it. Then Marley died and we were invited to the funeral service at the National Arena. Dressing for the occasion I had a head-wrap and a white caftan, and Gary gave me a little black heart that I pinned to my dress, and he was dressed similarly in white.

About half an hour after the funeral began, it suddenly hit me that this was what I had seen — Rasta colours draped around the Arena, but all the Rastas in white, and on the platform, bishops from the Ethiopian Orthodox Church. I turned to look at Gary at the same time he turned to look at me. And he said, "Well, this is what you dreamt about."

When my son Moyo died in London in 2007 I believe I felt him saying goodbye. In Kingston half-asleep in the wee hours of Saturday the ninth of June, I thought I was about to die. It's like a funny feeling took over my whole body, but the focal point was the pit of my stomach, my belly-bottom. You know how you hear a mother say *har belly-bottom tek har* when something happens to her child? When I finally picked up the phone to call for help I felt like a sort of coldness, a sort of calm, a sort of quiet passed over my whole body and the awful sinking sensation in the bottom of my tummy suddenly eased up. And I fell asleep. But when we got the terrible news that Moyo had been found dead in his apartment in London, the medical examiner estimated he had died just about the time I had been having these strange feelings in Jamaica.

These days my dreams are not as vivid as they used to be. They are like lantern slides, pictures flashing by quickly and most times in silhouette. Sometimes I can recognize a face or figure, but most times it's just a situation. Or I might hear a conversation in my head, as though it's just outside my window — but there's nobody out there. I recognize the voices, the mood, but I can't hear the words. I know who the people are and as soon as it begins to happen I'll remember — *I dreamt that.*

I've never felt I was meant to be like the four or five "gifted" people who suggested I develop my potential to be a psychic. But I have an unusual connection with my children, family members and close friends, and I know I have had experiences and perceptions that might be considered paranormal.

Chapter Ten

Return to JBC

After Australia I returned to JBC in 1970 and joined the television staff. There were hardly any local programmes. I worked with Bari Johnson on some, such as *Sweet and Lovely* and *Ai Zuzuwah*. We started *Ring Ding* in 1971. Somebody who should have known better had doubted whether Miss Lou could sustain half an hour on air. Bari and I got some children together in studio with Miss Lou, and with Marjorie Whylie on the piano, and we taped the proceedings. One memorable Saturday, the usual reel of foreign cartoons was somehow miraculously misplaced and we put on *Ring Ding* instead. The switchboard jammed with positive responses. Management was displeased, but in the end they decided to call the whole Saturday morning slot *Ring Ding* and include *Romper Room* (which already had sponsors).

When I left for Australia in 1968 there were two filing cabinets in my JBC office with edited tapes and master tapes. When I came back nobody seemed to know where to find the cabinets and the tapes. Then one day I was passing the rubbish heap where the incinerator was and I saw a whole stack of tapes, and sure enough some of them were in that pile. A new programmes manager brought from London had cleared the library. Many valuable tapes got thrown away in the 1970s. JBC lost so much.

In 1972 I was promoted to be head of JBC FM. I really didn't want to be an administrator. Carey Robinson, who was general manager at the time, put the challenge to me. While I was supposed to be thinking it over, equipment arrived and people were calling to ask where it should go. So by default I took on the gigantic project. Rupert Linton was the first operator, and Dermot Hussey helped me work out a music format that would make sense for us in Jamaica. We started by getting tapes from abroad – huge three-hour spools, mainly from a studio in California called CNB. Then we would do our own selection of records, 11:00 a.m. to 1:00 p.m. I gradually introduced UWI programmes and material from the BBC, Voice of America and Canadian Broadcasting: plays, poetry, biographical features and so on. From time to time we'd tape a school choir or concerts at the School of Music, or present a stereo recording of a TV special, such as at Easter or Christmas. Between six and eight in the evenings we aired a classical music programme, a jazz programme, and folk music from around the world.

People liked what we were doing. We offered many kinds of music and not a lot of talk. A couple of surveys gave us about 75 percent of the FM audience. RJR copied our format and made it work, while we systematically destroyed ours.

In 1975 Dwight Whylie, who was then general manager, asked me to try and do something about AM radio's poor listenership — only 12.8 percent at the time. I suggested a retreat in which a small group of us, including Charles Hyatt and Uriel Aldridge, would examine what JBC Radio had been doing and discuss ways to improve it. At a meeting early in 1976 — February, I think — it was agreed that the new format would be launched in May. Night after night, my living room became a work station, with things spread out everywhere and people like Dermot Hussey and Baldwin Lennon dropping in. Then Dwight Whylie left JBC and the acting general manager, Tino Barovier, wanted to know why there had not yet been any announcement of my appointment to the job I was actually doing. I went for lunch on a Friday and when I came back the place was in an uproar because Tino had announced that I was the director of JBC Radio I and 2. A lot of people who had been willing to pitch in and help until four, five, six in the morning all of a sudden took the line —"Is fi-har work, is she a get pay fi it." We could have accomplished more if I had not been officially appointed.

I struggled on from 1976 to 1978 in the role of director. Listenership increased and we knew we were on the right path, but there was resistance. No one seemed to want to have a woman in charge, and also there was political pressure to promote the party in power in preference to presenting national issues, the country's issues. I gave up that position and was asked to establish a theatre department by Wycliffe Bennett, the next appointee in the rapid turnover of JBC general managers. He kept saying that there cannot be a proper broadcasting service without a theatre department. There were no guidelines to follow, no real office, and at first no staff except me. I begged the administration to rent space across the road, I begged furniture from various places, and then, remembering what I could of the BBC system and the Australian system and what I knew of our situation here, I set up the new department.

The first thing I produced was a soap opera which management hoped might pull the mid-morning audience from RJR. It had been many years since we had a local soap opera on JBC and we thought the climate was right for another. Charles Hyatt (who joined me on the staff) persuaded Carmel Christie to write it, and we got to work. We cast it and started rehearsing. It took a little time to get off the ground and there were complaints about how we were spending money on the serial and it wasn't bringing in any revenue. But by the end of the first year, the serial *Floralee* had a sponsor and everything seemed rosy. At its largest, our staff consisted of Charles, Irma Parke, Ruth Ho Shing, Rosemarie Hudson and me. We did television plays as well, and we continued to use material from the BBC Transcription Service and our sources overseas which we thought might be of interest in Jamaica. It was going fairly well.

Then Wycliffe Bennett was manoeuvred out, and with him management support for the Department of Theatre. We had no budget to speak of, could not afford talent fees for acting or script writing; could not even get time in the editing room. By the end of 1979 I knew it was time to go.

On a freelance basis, I continued some of the programmes I had been doing, and then six months after I left JBC I was free to appear on RJR also. I did television work, commercials, the odd part in a film from abroad, and some teaching. I taught at the Caribbean Institute of Mass Communications (CARIMAC), the United Theological College (UTC), and did a lot of Festival work with the Jamaica Cultural Development Commission (JCDC). For many years I was their principal adjudicator in theatre and speech, travelling around the island, seeing everything. Eventually they separated theatre and speech, and I stayed with speech.

For a few months, beginning in November 1984, Lindy Delapenha and I co-hosted JBC TV's first live morning programme. We were promised features on Jamaica for *Morning Time* — we expected a team to be travelling around the country talking to interesting people. Instead we had to live with constant repeats; I got to know many of the *Health Watch* programmes by heart. Also the equipment was shabby — cameras would break down, microphones and the air conditioning would break down. Because Lindy was on staff, they wouldn't pay him anything extra for doing the early morning programme day after day; and eventually he said he wouldn't do it anymore. I was doing the show by myself for a while and I said, "Look, if I'm going to do the programme alone you'll have to pay me a little more." In hosting that programme for JBC, I was giving up potential income from RJR and commercials, and I hoped that *Morning*

Time could arrange something to compensate, maybe more freelance work for JBC. There was no meaningful response. Then I had a bad attack of sinusitis because a new studio was being built and the place was full of dust. The doctor gave me antibiotics but explained that they would make my face puffy. I wasn't willing to be seen on television with my jaw swollen and my eyes looking bleary. As my telephone wasn't working properly, I sent JBC a telegram to explain that I needed to be on sick leave for a week. When I was ready to return, Gloria Lannaman – the latest in the passing parade of general managers – said JBC had made other arrangements. That was the end of that.

Forbidden

I Marcus Garvey

My Son's Friend

Chapter Eleven

Doing *Old Story Time*

*P*eople sometimes ask me how I prepare for a role. Though at the first reading you may think, *Tremendous!*, you really have no idea what the character is going to ask of you until you start rehearsing and realize that most of it is not written in the words, and you start to think about the emotional guns you are going to have to fire.

For Trevor Rhone's *Old Story Time* we spent many hours talking about Miss Aggy, where she comes from, the whole setting of the play, all these people. In the Jamaican setting I know Miss Aggy, know lots of Miss Aggys, I know the Pa Bens and I know all the other people. I went to school with a Miss Pearl.

About Miss Aggy — I asked myself some questions. Is this just one woman I know or is it a composite of all the Miss Aggys I know? And how am I going to get it? Because if she is not totally convincing, she's going to make the play farcical, which it isn't. What really made the woman tick, that could make her come round at the end and say I'm sorry and I was wrong? It's difficult to say I was wrong and I'm sorry, and I thought this would give me a bit of a problem.

We had to examine the business of obeah. I believe but I don't believe. I don't think I would be going off to an obeah man to do anything I don't want — to have a bath or anything — but at the same time I am not prepared to dismiss obeah, because I have seen evidence of it. I have had weird experiences myself so I'm sort of a believing unbeliever, or maybe a believing non-practitioner. I spent hours with Trevor going into this. Even the chant at the end — he never told us until either very close to opening night or after opening night that it was in fact a real one from somewhere in Africa. And one of the things that happened was we noticed when we started playing — the first month or so — that the play more or less worked but something wasn't quite right, till Charles Hyatt said, "Look, the circle is going the wrong way." And we said, "Come, Charlie, how can it be going the wrong way?" And he said, "The circle going the wrong way. Check it." We changed the direction we were going, and believe me, after that the thing took off. It's one of those things I will never be able to explain, I don't think. If you look at the text and you look at what we do, there isn't very much there, and yet people got absolutely spellbound, and we got carried away. I used to be as cold as ice while they were trying to get out the devil. It was a weird experience.

Coming to terms with Miss Aggy and Pa Ben, getting rid of ourselves, Charles and I used to find that we needed all of two hours on performance day. We used to arrive within minutes of each other, roughly two and a half hours before the show began, and we would start talking, not as Leonie and Charlie but as Pa Ben and Miss Aggy, and whatever we related about the day, whether it was at JBC or the Carib or the market, it was related to those two people. And we found that by the end of the period we were ready.

I had a ritual with Miss Aggy. I had a cut-off point at 4:00 p.m. After that I didn't make much sense to anybody, and sometimes I was rather rude and very irritable and not pleasant to deal with, even when I was at work. Most people around me knew that. I'd snap and they'd say, "Rahtid, it's four o' clock. Leave her alone, mi love. Is Miss Aggy time." Or, "Is Old Story Time." And I'd get the bits and pieces ready. There's a bag that I used to pack. Everything in it had to be in its place. Then we would get to the Pegasus, and the things would come out in a certain order. When it dawned on me what I was doing, I laughed; but I didn't change it, because it seemed to work. She'd first get her underthings on, then her *crepe* and her socks, then her hair which had a net and a special way to do it. And then I would sit and watch my face become hers while we were talking with Pa Ben, who was doing the same thing. So by the time the rest of the cast arrived, it would be "Evening, Miss Aggy" and "Evening, Pa Ben". It was very seldom "Hi, Leonie" or "Hi, Charles", no matter what time they got there, and that used to do something for me. I thought, *Good*. And it meant too that any night you were not feeling your best there was always that to pull on, there was this solid something that would help you through.

I can remember one evening checking a door that was giving trouble, and saying to the stage manager, "If you don't fix this door it will fall tonight and spoil the whole thing." And he said, "I'll get it fixed." So I said, "Let me check it. Your fix and my fix is not the same." And having checked it, and feeling satisfied, I was charging off and the thing slipped and tore ligaments in my left foot. Charles had just walked in. I watched this great lump coming up on my foot and I was thinking, *But that's not my foot. What's going on?* I remember being picked up, taken off to the doctor, being given a painkiller injection, having the foot strapped, and getting back to the theatre, all in good time. When the curtain went up, it was just that Miss Aggy had a limp. But the pain went, she didn't feel it, and she was almost muttering to herself, "Damn ole rough road, de rockstone-dem, dem wouldn even fix it, if de bwoy-dem did break de rockstone little finer mi wouldn twist mi foot." She lived with that limp for about two weeks, but it never stopped anything.

I went through a period when I wished I hadn't said yes I'd do it. I think, with most roles that I come to love or that seem to do something to me careerwise, there's always a point when I want to run a hundred miles from it. I usually say to my director, when I trust him, "Look, when the point comes where I start finding excuses for backing out, don't let me, 'cause if you do, I'll come out." It's a horrible feeling, it's like I'm terrified, and if I begin to sense emotional tie-ups with the character I want to come out. I want to know why I'm not staying at my yard and putting up my feet and going off to a nice show or going to see my friends or something. And I'd say, "Look, I don't think I know this role." A mint of excuses. But if the director is like Trevor, he would just say, "Ten thirty tomorrow morning" or "Six o' clock tomorrow evening", ignoring me totally. Then I'll live through that period, fretting and sweating because I think maybe I'm not going to make it believable, maybe they're going to see bits of me in it, or bits of another character in it. That terrifies me. I don't want that to happen at all. Then that will pass. I'll begin to get excited, because the bits are falling into place.

I wasn't sure what Miss Aggy would look like. I knew she was older than I was looking at the time. But Aunt G had a friend who came to see her, and I thought, "Christ! That's Miss Aggy, Miss Aggy looks like that!" Aunt G thought I was being very rude, she called me inside and said, "How could you sit down staring on the woman like that?" I said, "Because her face looks just like the character." I got pencil and paper and started sketching the lines that the lady had, then I realized that it wasn't so much lines or anything like that, it's what was coming from inside the lady. Then I thought, *Well, you think all old people have wrinkles? She doesn't, and she will soon be eighty.* I sat and watched her. And I gave Aunt G a lift to visit the lady so I could have a look. Then now, on the inside, things had a face. Then I started thinking about what she would wear and why, and then I'd start watching people, we'd go out to the country and while I'm there I'm looking, and I thought, *Eh, eh. Oh yes. So she need a little space because she have a corn from all that walking up and down to market, and because she is a proper lady, she couldn't wear the ordinary frilly nice things we wear nowadays, and the bra couldn't be half-bra at all because that's a fancy modern thing.* Had to go and find a long-line one. I think I beg one off Aunt G or the children's grandmother. And it would begin to come together like that.

So she had a face. I thought, *What about her hair? All right, she's one of those ladies that would talk about "good hair", therefore if it have a little quality she going to do something that would show it, because she would want them to know she don't have no "burry" head, you know what I mean.* Bit by bit, it would come like that, closer and closer to opening night.

Then the nerves start. It's like all the ends started jangling at the same time and I'm terrified that it's not going to work but at the same time I want to try. We get down to opening night. It opens and fabulous things happen. At the end of it all, it's like a whole bucket of ice-water at the end of that ritual thing and when the eyes open — and sometimes I swear I'm not aware of stopping and opening my eyes — I'm just hearing this chant, and all sorts of things happen and it's like, oh, you know when you have been very hot, you've had a hot cup of coffee and that sort of heat and coolness that comes one and the same time, and I think, *Wow!*, and then you hear a sound and realize, *Oh, there's an audience!*

When you get comfortable in the role — like three, four, five, six months into the run, when you no longer have to worry about the lines that you are given by the author, they are going to come anyway — you begin to listen to the music some more. Is that the best possible way that line can go to convey precisely what you mean — not just what I mean but what it means in terms of the play. Then you begin what I call the finetuning, and things are timed out so precisely, and every night there's a little extra added.

I was once asked if I don't get bored after a long time, and I said, "But how can I?" I can't afford to, because it has to be new every night. If it's not new, the audience won't be impressed. And I'm not going to get bored and feel as if I've cheated, because in a funny kind of way I haven't yet learnt to deal with the praise and the "fabulous" and "fantastic" and "wonderful" and those nice warm things. I like it, I feel a split-second niceness, but what I really want to do is to hide away from all that. If I don't feel inside that I have either gotten to the point or I am pretty near, it really doesn't matter what anybody says. Though I say, "Thank you very much, very kind of you, I'm glad you enjoyed it," I want to go home to start digging into the performance, because it's like my performance is on a cassette and I will play it over and over. People say I don't call to them on the road. If I'm going to the theatre I never will, because I don't see them or hear them. I'm aware of the traffic and things. But if a scene didn't go so well last night, there was a little timing that was off, or you plan for a laugh — Trevor writes that way to give the audience release — and it didn't come off, I want to know why. So maybe two, three o'clock in the morning it's still going round in my head. I sleep, I wake up, it's there in my head, but you have a job to do. And this playing back can be dangerous.

I remember that one night in *Mother Courage* I "dried" (forgot my lines). It was like mentally I went flip, flip, flip, flip, and every time I get to that page it's blank! I thought, This is ridiculous. Fortunately it wasn't an actual performance, it was like about two rehearsals away from dress rehearsal. I am saying, *But this is so crazy, I know this role, so why am I drying up at this point and why can't I say anything?* Went home, found the script. The scripts had been photocopied, and because we had worked so hard at that particular spot the text was erased.

I guess I have a visual memory, but it's like my head is programmed. If the play is going to close on 30th January, don't ask me to do it on the 31st, 'cause chances are I won't remember very much. People like Bobby Ghisays, Lloyd Reckord, Bari Johnson could do miles of quotes, any play, anything. Don't bother with me and that, you know. I hear it, I know it, and sometimes I can say it with whoever is doing it, but for me to get up and spout an extract from this or that, it never happens, I can't. It's like it's been erased and I'm ready for the next imprint, or implant or whatever. If I have to do it, it will come back quickly. Like once when I'd been out of *Old Story Time* for about six months, I was asked on Saturday to do a show on Tuesday.

I went to the show on Sunday afternoon and I read through the script several times. There was no on-stage run-through but I did a word rehearsal at my home of some of the scenes with Karl Binger and Pauline Kerr who were playing Len and Lois. When the curtain went up on Tuesday I performed and I didn't miss a single word or anything.

You get a kind of high when you feel you've really achieved something on a given night. It's like you are standing in the wings and believe the person on stage has nothing to do with you. The audience laughs at the right places and they stop because they want to hear, and you hear people saying, "Sshh, hold down!" and so on, and, honestly, it's a physical force I feel. It's like something I can almost touch. It's like it's beginning to collect at the beginning of a performance and I'm thinking they're cold and suddenly there's an outburst of some sort and I begin to feel this thing and it builds and it builds and at the end it presents itself to me as whole. There are occasions when it feels like ninety-five or ninety-eight; on the rare occasion when I hit the hundred, absolutely nobody has to tell me. And usually the rest of the company feels it and we come off and say, "Hey! We really socked it to them tonight!" Or, "We deh deh!" Or halfway through we say, "Go deh, man! We getting there!" Or, "Off and running!" All little foolish phrases, but we know what we mean. Sometimes if you play 600 performances it mightn't be until the 575th that everything is right and you get that moment. And when that happens I feel kind of warm and I feel extra cool and it's like all the nerves are going, but in a very nice way, and it's easy to smile, it's easy to laugh, I don't really feel hungry, I don't feel tired anymore and I could go and do another show. It's like I've been recharged and regenerated.

Sometimes a performance goes unbelievably well. The final performance of *Old Story Time* at Carifesta 1981 in Barbados was one of those. After the show the Trinidadian actor Errol Jones, whom I hadn't met before, came backstage and just swept me off my feet and said, "Lawd, Miss Leonie! Lawd!" and I thought, *Yes*. And Joy Scott walked in and the tears were streaming down my face, and she said, "You told me it would be different, and I didn't believe you, but it was." I even get goose pimples now when I think about that performance. I had just lost a very dear friend who in the midst of his desperate illness had kept urging me to go to Carifesta. A number of things had been happening, and I thought people were being vicious, and I thought, *Leave them Carifesta alone, I don't want to go, I can't tek them kas-kas and bodderation*, and he kept saying, "No, man, you have to go, you have to go." And when I saw him the day before we left he said, "Go deh, Miss Lee! Sock it to them!" and I said, "Gwaan, I see you when I come." He died the day after we left and I heard like the Monday before we opened in Barbados, and that shattered me, and then I remembered him saying, "When something happens just take it into yourself, and if you must do something about it then make the performance be for the person." So it could be that the whole series of performances at Carifesta was a way of saying something, I'm not sure what. But it also meant I had good control of myself as a performer, because nobody would have guessed that I was really shattered. This was a person who, if I'm sitting at my office and I'm feeling depressed, or something happens or I have a bad headache, I hear footsteps and I look up and it's him, saying, "Come, Miss Lee, you want to cheer up." Or "How's the head?" or something. He never missed anything that I did, and if he said, "Look, that's good," I don't worry about it anymore, because he could be very critical and I trusted him. So his death was a shattering experience for me. And maybe all of that went into the Carifesta performance. I think that happens a lot, not just in my life but in the experience of a number of performers — when you suffer emotional trauma you take the energy from the pain and the loss and the confusion or whatever it is, and turn it right around, and it gives you an extra something that I think is difficult to define, but somebody might just notice that tonight you are exceptional, you are finely tuned. I mean, like everything is working tonight! You feel a kind of charge that will make you instinctively do the right thing. You can have rehearsed the timing so that the moment will always be convincing, but the performance that tears at your heartstrings only happens when everybody's firing.

There were a couple of performances at the Pegasus that went very well, and the last one in Toronto. At that last show in Toronto, when we hit the stage for the curtain call it was like a football match, like Cup Final at Wembley —

the people just got up and roared, and it's like I never wanted to move from there, but at the same time I wanted to disappear, because I thought, *Christ, this can never be re-peated, and let me not get this stuck in my head in case I think that this is how it's going to be, for this is a once in a lifetime thing.*

When it doesn't go well I also know. All sorts of things can go wrong. One of the actors may get a bad "dry", or a prop may be out of place or the door doesn't work at the right time, or a blackout is too late or too early. Or it can be that my costume needs washing and I've forgotten to say, or that they promised to wash it and didn't do it, or I'm aware that instead of a zipper I have pins, and I'm worried about how I'm going to get out of the costume and into the next set of clothes. Sometimes it's so silly: like I've forgotten the mint ball in my pocket and the money for Pa Ben is stuck to the wet mint ball so I have to fight to get it out. Or the switch breaks when it shouldn't, because somebody forgot to put a fresh one there, or I hit the stage and suddenly realize I don't have my pencil and the leaves. Whose fault is that? Mine. I was chatting backstage and didn't remember to put the thing in my head. And then you have to work ten times as hard to get the concentration back. Or somebody jumps a crucial line or moves and creates a diversion at an important moment and you have hell to get it all together again and the whole performance that night remains mediocre, just that much away from being memorable, because some-one moved, someone coughed or crackled paper or made a comment that everybody else heard.

And yet there are times when the odd comment can do some of your work for you, it can release something in the audience, make them forget themselves and relax. You hear some women bawl out, "Wicked!" or "But see ya!" and you sense a kind of freedom after that, it's as if they kicked off their shoes and said, "Now let's really go with this thing," and you romp home after that.

If the show goes very badly, whether it's my fault or not, when I go home I want to cry, I want to hide, I don't want to see anybody or anything. I just want to get home, have a drink or have a cup of tea or just go to bed.

When it goes well, I'm still not particularly keen on the "Oh darling, what a wonderful show!" — that's not really me, I still want to take it into myself. I'll share it with the children or a few close friends. We might go and have a drink and I'll say, "Cho, come to the yard." Or you might stand in the yard talking and you feel good, you feel you did your very best and it worked. But it's very seldom that I think there's nothing else to do, and the better it goes the more work I have, to find how else can I make it better. Like I think, *This line is funny but they usually chuckle, they don't laugh. What can I do with it?* Or I might say to the other performers, "Let us try so and so, check it with the director." Then if we do it and it works, that means we play it that way tomorrow night, and find something else to re-examine.

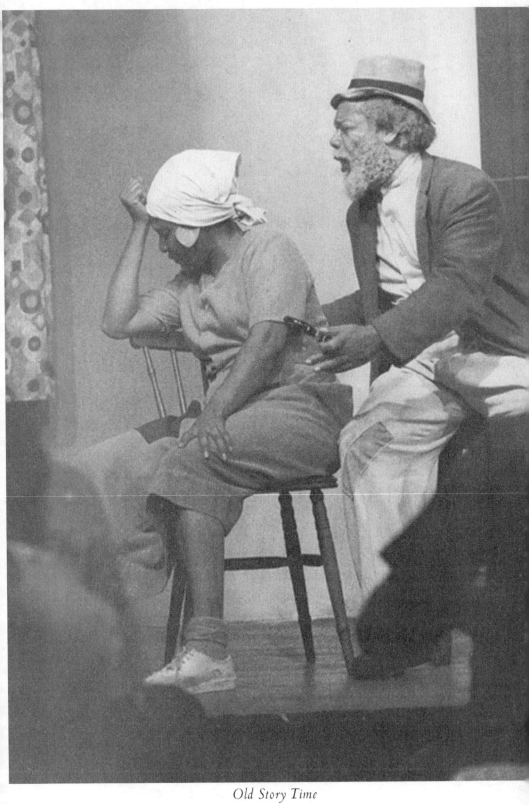

Old Story Time

Old Story Time

Old Story Time

Chapter Twelve

Some Other Challenges

In every medium, the challenge to the actor is fundamentally the same: how to create the character you are playing, in voice and body language which seem to know and feel the character's history. Preparation is essential. The more you understand the better.

In live theatre the audience response is an essential element, varying from show to show. Though the professional actor may achieve a high degree of consistency, no two performances are exactly the same, and you create each performance moment after moment. For film you may do repeated takes of various scenes, in any order, and some of your best work may be edited out. In *Club Paradise* I had two scenes with Peter O'Toole and, in the breaks, some lovely conversations about Britain and RADA and all that. But when the film came out, I was missing. Same thing with Charlie Hyatt and Louise Bennett – they had a lot of fun with Robin Williams which didn't make it to the final version.

What My Mother Told Me, a film by Frances-Anne Solomon, was a terrific experience. It was shot in sequence, so when it called for dawn we were up at three thirty and sitting on that jetty waiting for the sun to come up so we could catch it at the right time. The team actually lived for a while in the house that was the set. Frances-Anne and Ajoua (who played my daughter) and I worked on improvisations to get what Frances-Anne wanted. Emotionally I was dried out at the end of it all. I don't think I could have gone another week. Part of the tension was because of what I was not allowed to do in reacting to Ajoua. In the quarrel scene she said some horrible things and I was not allowed to say a single word, so that when my chance to break out came I was ready to kill her.

I love the sea and will sit by it for days on end. But I don't like boats — I can't swim, I don't feel safe. When I told Frances-Anne, she reminded me that my character was not afraid. After my fights with Ajoua I was supposed to take her out in the boat because I now understand a little bit more about her, and we are to be happy and laughing. I got the man who owned the boat to help me. He stayed in the boat, out of sight, to rescue me if necessary. In the end I was glad to have confronted my fear.

In the film *Children of Babylon* I had to play Dorcas, a character who says nothing but must communicate exactly what she means. It's not so much that Dorcas was dumb as that Dorcas never spoke, nobody ever asked her anything and waited for a reply. Besides, nobody knew where she came from. She didn't have any family. She only had Luke to relate to — that's why he could hurt her so badly that she would kill herself. I know some Dorcases — the symbolic Dorcas and the real Dorcas.

Lennie Little-White, the director, pointed out that I was the only pro in the company and said he was expecting me to help him hold them together. I'm not sure we succeeded, but for me *Children of Babylon* was nice. It asked things of me I never thought I'd be doing at any time, let alone on film. Lennie raised hell when I didn't want to take off the top for the painting for Rodney. I did it, and that scene in bed, and the one outside the door when feelings tek me over because I was peeping at the people inside.

It was very hard work. There was one scene when Dorcas was so emotionally upset and so many things were going to happen to her, and I knew that if I uttered a sound it would ruin everything. When the production manager came calling to say it was time for us to have breakfast and move out — this must have been about five thirty in the morning — I thought I had answered him, but for that whole day not a sound came out of my throat until the scene was filmed. Lennie had three versions in the can, and somewhere way down in the afternoon when I was offered a cup of mint tea I was telling the lady, "Yes, thank you," and suddenly realized not a sound had come out. Lennie said, "That's why we have you in the film, because you tek this thing serious." They thought I just wouldn't speak. Only Chappie St Juste realized I couldn't speak. I was getting set to go racing into Montego Bay to the doctor and write "HELP" because my voice had gone, as far as I knew. But it came back.

Though you are better paid for doing film, I prefer the emotional rewards of live theatre. I think my most successful roles have been Miss Aggy in *Old Story Time*, Mother of Judas in Easton Lee's *The Rope and the Cross* and Ojuola in Rotimi's *The Gods Are Not to Blame*.

My entry into serious theatre was in a Barry Reckord play, *Miss Unusual*, in 1956. I had been typing the script for him, and he said, "Would you like to be involved with the production?" I said, "Yes, as what?" He said, "You could be the prompter, and you could help with the props." In the end Lloyd Reckord, who was directing, asked me to understudy the leading character, Miss Unusual.

Shortly after the opening there was a show for which the leading lady was unavailable, so I had to go on. After performances at the Ward Theatre and at the Old Dramatic Theatre at the university, Lloyd decided to take it around to some cinemas as a curtain raiser before the feature film. We did it at State and then at Tropical. Unfortunately for me, the reverend gentleman in charge of the church Aunt G and I attended saw me at Tropical, and disapproved of me kissing and all that on stage. As it happens, *Miss Unusual* closed not long after that.

As a result of working with Lloyd in *Miss Unusual* he invited me to audition for *Busha Bluebeard*, the first pantomime I took part in. *Busha Bluebeard* and the Ivy Baxter dancers went down to Trinidad for the West Indian Festival of Arts in 1958 – a whole planeload of us.

I had a mishap in a pantomime, *Queenie's Daughter*. About two weeks before it opened I was racing across the courtyard and fell and twisted my ankle very badly, so it had to be strapped up. We opened on Boxing Day as usual and got to the middle of January. The opening set was a ship, with a ramp that went off into the wings and steps leading from the ramp to the stage floor. This particular performance, I came flying off but there were no steps – someone had moved them – and there was no bulb in the work light on that huge column backstage. I stepped into thin air and came down heavily on that same damaged left ankle. A member of the cast took me back to the dressing room but I still had to go on, so in a kind of numbness I went on for a short scene, came off, and they yelled for a doctor in the house. Dr Owen Minott happened to be there, and he had bandages and so on in his car, so the ankle was strapped stiff with boots and everything on. I finished the performance and went to the hospital, was given morphine, and did x-rays. I never went back to the production – I couldn't, because even after it had healed, I had about six months of physiotherapy before the ankle was useful again. I had badly torn ligaments.

I've been in a number of Shakespeare productions. My *Merchant of Venice* Portia (done in Australia) was probably the best of my Shakespeare performances. I played Cleopatra when I was still at drama school in London – it was my graduating piece and we took it to other parts of England. In Jamaica I did Titania in a Paul Methuen open-air production of *A Midsummer Night's Dream*, with Bari Johnson as Oberon and Ranny Williams as Bottom. We opened in Montego Bay, at the old great house at Round Hill. The way the set was constructed, when Oberon and Titania and the fairies disappeared it looked as though we had gone off into the clouds over the sea. Perhaps because of Ranny, the production was well supported by a cross-section of people living in Montego Bay and nearby districts.

In other Paul Methuen productions I've been Maria in *Twelfth Night* and Katherina in *The Taming of the Shrew* (with Ranny Williams as Petruchio). I see Katherina as one of my big successes. But the day before we opened at Round Hill I came down with chicken pox. I had a temperature of 103° and itchy little nodules popping up all over me. I remember being driven into Montego Bay for an injection to get me through the afternoon. On top of all that, Madame

Soohih was killed in a car accident on her way to see the show. The whole thing was traumatic; it was a miracle I got through the performance. Sometimes in the afternoon sun I was so bleary-eyed from fever I could hardly see the people I was working with. Mas Ran as Petruchio got carried away and gave me the box of my life — I thought my jaw was dislocated. But the show went well. We delayed the opening in Kingston until I was better and the chicken pox blisters had dried up.

In England and Ireland I took part in a marvellous all-black production of Oscar Wilde's *The Importance of Being Earnest*, directed by Yvonne Brewster. We had only three weeks of rehearsal, from ten in the morning until five thirty or six in the evening. We opened in Newcastle Upon Tyne, and had a good run at the Bloomsbury Theatre in London.

The set suggested a railway station with a glassy-looking, translucent roof which became a conservatory in the country estate of Algernon, with a huge tree, and benches and plants. It was gorgeous. We had perfect costumes, and rehearsed from the very first day in our bum-rolls and boots, with our fans and the china for tea — rented, but genuine bone china, if you please.

We didn't change a word of the Oscar Wilde text, and we took pains to get the language and the accents right. Oscar Wilde's grandson and his daughter-in-law said it was the best production of the play they had seen in about twenty years. One reviewer said he couldn't think of an English actor who could have played Algernon as well as our leading man, Ben Thomas. (A couple of years later, Ben won the Best Actor Award – playing Macbeth, I believe.) Our Lady Bracknell was the celebrated Jamaican actress Mona Chin (Hammond). Dr Chasuble was Oscar James. I was Miss Prism.

In Edward Henry's *See Mama*, directed by Munair Zacca – in Kingston – I had a cameo performance as a lady in her sixties dying of cancer. A young man called Jacko played my son. The scene was set in Brooklyn, where she is packing her barrel to go home and saying what she hoped to find in Jamaica, and what had happened when she went to the doctor. One night I had a terrible dry, but because Jacko and I had built up a relationship, having spent hours talking to each other, he just kept talking, feeding me my own lines and his so naturally that not even the director, Munair, knew what had happened. The old lady had a habit of humming, from "Rock of Ages" through to "Abide with Me", and she was always mending something. So she was humming and mending until finally one word clicked, then two, then a whole sentence, and we were off and running again.

Munair suggested that, instead of staying in costume for the curtain call, I put on simple evening clothes and take off the wig. It was amazing: in spite of what the programme told them, night after night it was a while before the audience connected me with the old lady.

The Amen Corner (by James Baldwin) went very well. I can remember looking at the *Gleaner* reviewer Harry Milner and knowing that he was totally caught up towards the end of the play where the husband has died in Sister Margaret's arms, she gets back into the church to realize she has lost the leadership, and she disintegrates right there in the pulpit before her congregation.

The way Lloyd Reckord directed it, you had to hold that moment, making sure the audience is with you, because if they're not the whole play flops. He sent me centre-stage and had me just stay there. No traditional curtain call for Sister Margaret. People came on and bowed, and I just stayed there with a pin spot. And most nights it was very difficult to move from there, because it was like I had no energy, there was nothing left.

There was another part of the play too where her sister is saying, Look, you have to hold yourself together and not pay too much attention to these people, and Sister Margaret is saying, Look, I'm in trouble, because last night when I prayed, at the end of it all I couldn't say amen. According to the script, she is crying. During rehearsals no tears came, but once we started playing, people would let go, they opened up and gave. A lot of times my skill was not in making the moment believable but in not getting carried away by it — I mean, being able to stop, cut it off.

In *December*, by Patrick Brown, two elderly people express their mutual dependence by exchanging insults on the edge of death. Patrick asked me to play Titta Watson with Errol Jones as Ezra. The script in its original form was out and out comedy, but Errol and I and the director, Trevor Nairne, thought the production should highlight what we found real in the relationship of these two old people. Some things were cut from the script and some were interpreted differently from what Patrick may originally have intended.

Physically, *December* was not a nice play for me to do. My continual coughing as Titta ruined my ears, my throat, my chest. It took me about two months after the final performance to get my chest clear. I remember one night when I coughed and coughed and the coughing changed gear, I heard a lady in the audience say, "Lawd Jesus! Poor t'ing!" She came backstage afterwards to tell me of a remedy, something to do with aloe vera and granulated sugar and onions.

A German actor/playwright called Roland Reber started a World Theatre Project with support from UNESCO. Insisting that people are people, anywhere in the world, he said he'd had enough of killings and wars, and wanted to make a contribution to world peace. The idea was to develop an international team of performers who would travel and work together for a while. He brought some actors from Germany to Jamaica. Four Jamaicans — Glen Campbell, Denise Francis-Robinson, Steve Higgins and I — got involved, but after a while Denise and Steve had other commitments. Glen and I travelled to Germany and India with the project, working with other performers there.

One of the productions Reber pulled together in Jamaica was called *Beyond the Horizon*. Columbus and his men arrive somewhere new, ask no questions, take over the place, and they themselves change in the process of destroying people and their environment. The priest becomes the dictator, whom the professional soldier wants to replace. A prostitute marries a soldier but their dreams are not fulfilled. Soldiers go off to the hills to kill people for water. I played a mother who rails against God because her son has died in war. She may or may not be mentally disturbed. A lamb she takes into her arms is slaughtered by the enraged dictator, and she embraces the prostitute as her child. Audiences were captivated, especially by fighting done in slow motion and to classical music.

In preparing to do Brecht's *Mother Courage* I read a lot, and talked a lot with Germans, trying to find out how they thought, what they felt, what their reactions were, and feed all that into my mental computer. I asked the director, Norman Rae, to let me try a German accent, but he found that when the character got very upset, the accent got thicker and harder to understand. I said that was something I could work on, but he said no, there were already more than enough variations in accent. There were people in the cast who didn't handle standard English well.

As Sophie in Errol John's *Moon on a Rainbow Shawl* — a Drama Workshop production directed by Thom Cross — I did a Trinidadian accent which worked well. Keith Noel was Ephraim, Ed "Bim" Lewis was Charlie, Fae Ellington the young girl, Rosa. The lecherous landlord was played by my husband at the time, Keith Amiel.

The Rope and the Cross was written and directed by Easton Lee, who has been a friend for many, many years. Every Easter he used to involve me in a concert or a presentation of one sort or another in Siloah, St Elizabeth, to raise funds for the church. Then one year he wrote something based on his childhood memory of a conversation between his mother and another lady. He had heard one of them say, "Everybody talks about Mary the mother of Jesus; but Judas had a mother too." Easton asked me to play Miss Birdie, a very ordinary, down-to-earth, lively little lady selling saltfish fritters who falls asleep at a Good Friday service and dreams she is the mother of Judas.

Judas's mother turned out to be one of the largest and most terrifying characters I've ever played. Halfway through the first run of the play — and we used to do it at Easter-time in a number of different churches — I didn't know where I ended and this little woman took over. Sometimes I'd be coming down the aisle after she's found her son and sort of covered him, and it's like this woman is saying, "Come on, tell my story", and strange things were happening to me. On a number of occasions other members of the cast — Grace McGhie, perhaps, or Fae Ellington or Jean Rhone — would practically have to tear the mother's costume off me to get me back into the costume for Miss Birdie so I could go into the church and fall asleep. I couldn't understand, and then I thought I must be going off the deep end or something.

In the research I did I found out that Judas's mother wasn't a poor lady by any means, so she would have been well preserved, and she had Judas late in her life. It used to amaze me sometimes that, after Miss Birdie who was sort of nice and plump and round, and flat-footed, with her basket and head-tie and stuff, I would lose about thirty pounds when I took off her costume; and I suddenly felt long and thin and there was a slight curve in my back — I don't know how it got there, I didn't consciously do it.

One run we had the last performance at St Andrew Parish Church and by the time it was finished I was so broken, so distraught, so utterly identified with this woman that I didn't want to see anybody, not even the parson who wanted to say thank you to us. It was as if there was a whole world of stuff bottled up inside and wanting to come out and the only chance it got was when I found the boy and was saying how Judas was as a child. I had no problem weeping bitter tears at that point. I'm now dead scared of that role – maybe I think I could go into it and not come out again.

The Gods Are Not to Blame, by Ola Rotimi, is the Oedipus story transposed to fifteenth-century Nigeria. It is an epic sometimes mounted with hundreds of actors. Yvonne Brewster's UK production had just twelve (six men, six women) performing on a drum-shaped cow-skin set, only fifteen feet in diameter, and lit from underneath so that the actors looked like porcelain figures. The lighting was done by an expert from the Royal Opera House.

Almost everything used in the production was authentic. Yvonne spent time in Nigeria and brought back all the props, including a shrunken monkey's head that the king wore. The men had to shave their heads, the girls had huge head-dresses or intricate braids with cowrie shells. The cast had to learn to wear their wraps so they could move easily in them, kneeling, rising and so on. There were no drummers, no musicians other than the cast of twelve, but we made our own sounds.

The Oedipus figure, Odewale, was played by Jeffrey Kissoon, a powerful actor from Trinidad nicknamed "Issa" who had a kind of raw magnetism. I played his mother, Ojuola. One of the extraordinary moments in the production was when Ojuola realizes that her new husband, Odewale, is actually her son. She calls on the gods, makes a split-second connection with Odewale, then everything stops and she walks all the way round the circle. The high priestess from the back of the stage then begins a song that's picked up by the rest of the cast as the lights begin to change. Ojuola glances at Odewale again, connects with him and takes the final decision to kill herself.

She goes to the altar, picks up the dagger, makes a terrible sound, gets up and walks at the rim of the circle stage to almost opposite to where she was, and as she goes different members of the cast begin a sort of dirge which is picked up by others. By the time she stops walking, you know she has done it. When I read that moment in the script I thought, *Dear Lord, how do I do this?* Because that sound has to say everything – the discovery, the despair, the shattering of everything she knows. The sound I used tore me apart every time. It came to me from a night when there had been shooting in the ghetto behind my house – a baby got shot through the head – and I heard a woman saying, "Laaaaaawd! Mi baby dead!" and repeating that devastated sound.

Odewale goes numb when he realizes he has married his mother. The lighting changes and you see a great hole where his mouth used to be and the whole place is bathed in red. All the actors on the stage are in tears and you could hear a sniffle from the audience. Then the yards and yards of silk folded on stage at the beginning of the play are picked up by me (Ojuola) when I fall and I'm wrapped in it. Odewale takes the other end and goes with it, suggesting that there's all that blood tying him and me, until it stops exactly in the middle of the stage, and everything again is bathed in red. Many nights it was not until we were halfway through the curtain call that you would hear any audience reaction, then resounding applause would erupt.

The theatre critics were enthusiastic. and the playwright, Rotimi, brought to London by the British Council for the opening night, said he was thrilled. Accustomed to huge productions with hundreds of performers, including be-feathered drummers and all that, he could hardly believe the powerful theatre he had witnessed in spite of the numerically small cast. He said it gave him a new understanding of what he had written.

The Gods Are Not to Blame could be the most exciting and unusual thing I've done in the whole of my career. I've been in some wonderful productions, but this was to me like magic.

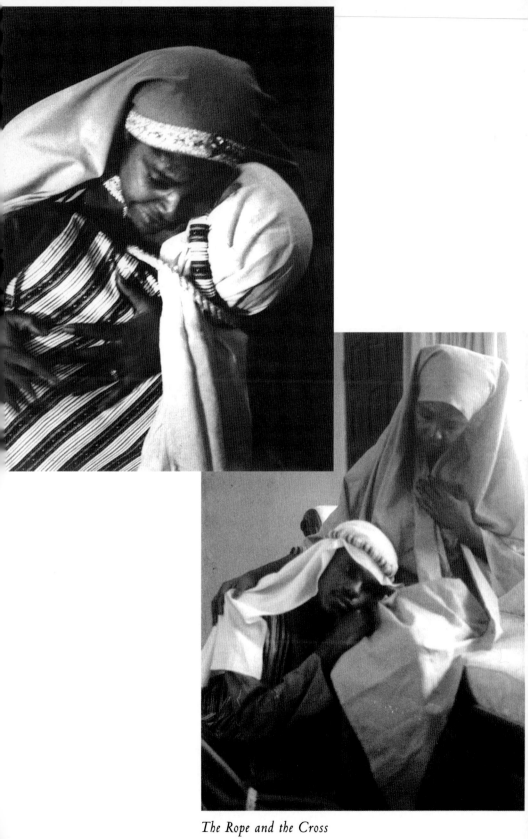

The Rope and the Cross

The Gods Are Not to Blame

What My Mother Told Me

December

The Importance of Being Earnest

The Taming of the Shrew

Children of Babylon

The Orchid House

Chapter Thirteen

Reflections

In my late teens I was very keen on church. I was a Sunday school teacher, but a couple of things happened and I said to myself, *This thing is not really for me.*

When I started working, I and some other girls would go down King Street, pool our funds and buy flowers to make the church pretty. One Friday I bought flowers for a special service on Sunday, took them to the church and arranged with the caretaker that on Sunday night after service we would parcel up the flowers and beg him take them to three or four people in hospital. We thought this would be nicer than just leaving them. At the end of the service we were heading up to the altar to collect the flowers when a church sister elbowed me aside. I said, "I'm sorry, I'm going for the flowers." She said, "Well, you haffi wait till me tek out what I want, den you can tek." I said, "But is I buy it!" She was mortally offended, but so was I.

Then there were one or two other things — such as a man calling me into the vestry to tell me that my lipstick too red, and that I should wipe it off; and finding that people I saw looking sanctimonious on Sunday would pass me on the road in the week and not talk to me. Gradually, I got turned off.

But I talk to God, you know. You won't hear any words. Like I'm saying, *Look here, this is so and so. I just saying if you just show me where to walk and what to go and do, then I will go and do this thing.* Sometimes when I wake up in the morning I feel a lot better about the problem, I just feel that things will be all right. Sometimes people hurt you and you feel as if your inside is falling out. Always, just before the curtain goes up, there's a moment with God, and my request is not to make me a star or make me brilliant, but help me to make the audience feel good. *Stay with us, go with us, make the whole thing go well so that it's worth it for them for the evening.* And I find that even if I'm shaking like a leaf I can perform. God is good.

I remember once going to Richmond Park Moravian Church — I ended up being confirmed in the Moravian Church — and I was broke, had only a couple of dollars in my purse. They were taking up a special collection for something, and I just gave what I had. By next afternoon I got a call to come and pick up a cheque I wasn't expecting. I find coincidences like that all the time — I'm down, I'm broke, but, *What the hell, you need a fifty cent or a fifty dollar, see it here.* And out of the blue something comes that gives me the returns about ten times over.

When I moved into a cottage off Barbican, Oliver Daley was the parson who did the prayers at the housewarming. He prayed the house would always have love, that people would be welcome and that when they came they would feel comfortable, feel the love, and it would make things a little better for them.

I don't visit a lot. I'm not comfortable in many homes, I can't stay long. I prefer my own place. Sometimes it's like I crawl in there and feel protected. People are welcome, but I find it harder to go out and take the world by storm. I die a thousand times when I have to go into a crowded room, and I do what I call my duchess act — I look for a face I know, or I take a deep breath and just sail in, and people think I'm so confident. Even at home, if too many people are there I begin to get edgy.

In a sense I'm not neighbourly. I'm not curious about what's going on over there, and sometimes I'm not sure I like it when people want to come in and do the neighbourly thing. When I go home I want to be with people I know well, so that I can relax, can think things through, or be miserable, or let my face hang down, or put my feet up, whatever.

The friends I value most are truthful and loyal. You might quarrel with them, but when it comes to certain things you can absolutely rely on them and they can rely on you. Whatever you do you don't let down your friend. I don't have many close friends; but those I have, matter. In fact, I've become friends to some of their friends.

My children mean everything to me. I was never the conventional mom, but I wanted to make them proud and to provide for them. Today they sustain me, being the people they have become. They now take charge when I am shaky. I learn from them, as they have learnt from me. They help me towards balance.

Robert lives in North Carolina with his wife, two children and a granddaughter. We do not see each other often, but we talk on the phone. He's doing well — works hard, is in touch with his Jamaican roots and has a great sense of fun. Born with a malformed kidney, he has defied the medical odds — living proof what faith can do.

Karen is insightful and full of new ideas. She is creatively energetic, loving and honest; digs into everything, wants it explained. She helps me choose and prepare my roles, and privately reviews my performances. Two strokes in 2005 left her physically challenged on one side, but she's had therapy and can now drive herself around. She and her husband live apart, but they care deeply for one another and are constantly in touch.

Moyo, who died so suddenly in London in 2007, was gentle, quiet, confident, with a wicked sense of humour. Technology was his thing: he could design and make his own computer. He was a reliable man who kept his commitments, in business and in personal life.

Dianne is strong, outgoing and witty — can be the life of any small gathering. Drawn to adventure and independence, she does not like to be pulled, pushed or pressured. She is

also very caring, does most of the phoning and the writing
and the e-mailing to keep the family together.

I think our Jamaica School of Drama should be doing more
to produce rounded performers. I don't think the students
understand enough about literature and the theatrical
traditions from other places. I'm not trying to say they
must overlook our own, but they should never be satisfied
until our graduates can go anywhere in the world and work.
We need actors capable of portraying Caribbean characters
and a range of other characters as well. My dissatisfaction
with many of our drama school graduates is that you give
them a kitchen sink or a backyard drama set in Jamaica and
they're home and dry, but put them in Trinidad or Barbados
or Guyana and they're lost. Many of them can't manage a
believable American accent. Many of them can't do what we
may call an upper St Andrew English accent. You can't do
justice to a play if it's written in standard English and you
can't speak standard English! The girls, even doing old-time
Jamaican plays, once you give them a long skirt and a fan
they're completely at sea, they don't know what to do. The
fellows can't do a ceremonial bow, can't make a leg, so to
speak — and that used to be done here in Jamaica too,
among the planters. If we're going to portray them then we
really ought to know about these things. Many of our students
know very little about the social graces, they don't know

which glass goes where, they don't know which fork to use when, so put them in a banquet scene and we'd be terribly embarrassed. In my drama training in England we had to practise holding a cigarette, sipping sherry, tasting wine, and all that, and exactly how to sit at table and what to say to whom – and we were made to buy little books to find out how different people should formally be addressed.

Also, many of our students can't sustain beyond maybe half a dozen performances an interpretation that they've worked on and set. They allow all sorts of things to colour their performance – somebody laughs tonight, and tomorrow night the actor's holding up the play waiting for the laugh, not realizing that it mightn't come, because it's a different audience.

I think a director should encourage actors to discover the characters they are playing. The actor is not a puppet. The best directors respect the talent, the intelligence, of actors they are working with. I like a director who will listen to any ideas you have that might enhance the production or help to clarify your character or a particular area of the play. I hate directors who expect a performance on the first day of blocking, and I will fight them. That kind of director drives me nuts. I say, "What is rehearsal for? We have to explore and experiment and so on. What you asking me to perform? I don't know the woman! I don't know a thing about her except how old she is and where she is. I haven't found out anything about her – this is the first day, for heaven's sake!" And I don't like directors who every five lines want to get up on stage and show you how to say the words. If you hire me to do the job, why are you doing it for me? I like the director who is thoroughly prepared, who arrives with a vision of the production but also leaves the actor room to explore. So that when the director says, "Let me see what you think," you can be sure that he or she is not relinquishing responsibility but wants to learn what you can do to strengthen the production. I am formulating ideas in my mind about the character and how I feel her fitting into things, but I need to know how the director sees the overall picture. I like when directors are firm, when they can explain why they want something a certain way, even if they are saying, "But the character wouldn't do this at this point." If there's a reason and they can explain it, I can deal with it. I also like if when I get a bright idea or I feel a certain way I can say to the director, "At this point I don't feel like this."

I myself am not cut out to be a director. I co-directed one pantomime, a revival of *Anancy and Pandora*, and that was it. I wanted to die when I saw people doing nonsense, and I didn't want to go up there and say, "This is how you do it." Some of the actors were playing around. They weren't serious. They come tonight and you have to make the same corrections you made last night. They haven't made notes. Two nights before the dress rehearsal you're having a technical run-through and the lighting man hasn't come, or he's stuck up two blue lights you really don't want. Then you're fighting with the costume people and the music people. I introduced a rehearsal schedule – at that time not the norm in pantomime productions – so that people didn't have to come night after night and waste time. If for any reason I had to be absent, somebody could take my book and conduct the rehearsals planned for that night. I found directing a terrible strain. I prefer to put the effort into my own performance.

Reviewers, critics – call them what you like – can be useful. Feedback can be of value, if you can trust the person offering it, if you believe them to be honestly reporting their response. I will not accept some people who have axes to grind, or who come late and then report on the whole thing and get it wrong. I do believe we need critics, but we need serious people who have knowledge and experience of theatre. Over the years I have been helped by knowledgeable friends – people such as Charles Hyatt, Bobby Ghisays, Ruth Ho Shing, Alma MockYen, Fae Ellington, Grace McGhie, Trevor Rhone, Bari Johnson and many others. Criticism from folks I trust can terrify me, and I will agonize for days, I will go into a blue funk, not because I'm upset but because I'm wondering, *How am I going to fix it?* For I myself am hardly ever satisfied with my performance.

Some of the people performing these days don't take their responsibilities seriously. They should be at the theatre an hour before the show – a minimum of half an hour if there's a good reason why they're as late as that. But some actors think it's all right to arrive ten minutes or a quarter of an hour before curtain time, when everybody else is fretting and wondering what's happened to So-and-so. Then they go on stage to perform. They haven't had any time to shed what's outside, let alone take on what's necessary for the production. Sometimes that's why things don't work so well. Or somebody comes to the theatre in good time for his eight-thirty show but sits in his car for an hour, and when he decides to go backstage he finds he has left his costume at home. At that point he needs to go home for it, so the curtain goes up fifteen minutes late.

When you take a production abroad, you add a whole series of challenges. Many of the promoters rent places that may be suitable for singers and musicians but not for a play. They have no idea what is required. They are puzzled when you ask for an ironing board for the costumes. To me it's as though they think you arrive and you just do it, or it just happens by itself. The venues they book are often not available to you before midday of the day that you are opening or, when you're lucky, ten thirty in the morning, and you haven't seen the place before. And, believe me, when you are through at night you're exhausted and they'll almost be locking you up in the place.

I can remember performing in New York without a set. I was angry about that. But I thought, *People are coming, so let's see what we can do*, and in fact they didn't seem to notice there was no set. But, for the actors, it was hell. You couldn't come off and wait for your cue, you were trekking miles back and forth offstage, and walking and running. And when you came off and went into the changing room, you couldn't stay there, it was just a strip of cloth. That sort of thing.

It can be very satisfying, though, to perform a Jamaican play abroad for an audience that is mainly Jamaican. They respond warmly to a little piece of home, especially when they know it can stand comparison with other plays being done out there.

God is good. I give thanks for family and friends, and the many people with whom I have collaborated in theatre, broadcasting and other endeavours. I am glad to have been allowed a rewarding range of roles. I have learnt from every aspect of my life.

*Receiving the Order of Distinction from
Governor General Sir Florizel Glasspole*

*With Prime Minister
Michael Manley and
Errol Jones*

*With astronaut
Ronald E. McNair on
Morning Time*

Accepting an award from Sheryl Lee Ralph

*With Geoffrey Gunther
and Trevor Rhone*

With Tanya Williams

Appendix 1

From Leonie's Resumé

Educational Background and Training

1961–63   *Royal Academy of Dramatic Art, London*
             (on scholarship)
             Diploma
             VC Buckley Award for style and wearing of costumes

1954–55   *Durham Commercial College, Kingston*

1951–54   *Excelsior High School, Kingston*
             9 subjects at Senior Cambridge (O' level)

1944 –51   *Kingston Senior School*
             First Jamaica Local

Work Experience

1979 to present   *Consultant/Lecturer*
                  Voice & speech and presentation techniques
                  Radio Education Unit – University of the West Indies
                  (UWI), Mona

Caribbean Institute of Mass Communications, UWI, Mona

United Theological College

Grace Kennedy Company Ltd.

Courts Jamaica Ltd.

Cable & Wireless Jamaica Ltd.

Credit Union League

University of Technology (UTECH)

Various hotels

Adjudicator
Jamaica Cultural Development Commission

Television and radio commercials
for the Jamaican, Caribbean, UK and USA markets

Compère
From state functions to school concerts, as well as
reading poetry and citations

1970–79   *Jamaica Broadcasting Corporation (JBC)*
Head of Department of Theatre
Director of Radio Broadcast
Head of JBC Radio 2 (first FM station in Jamaica)

1968–70   *IBM Australia Ltd.*
Secretary to Systems Engineers
Librarian

1966–68   *Jamaica Broadcasting Corporation (JBC)*
Producer/Presenter – Radio
Continuity and News – TV

1961–66   *Royal Academy of Dramatic Art (RADA)*
Radio, television and stage

1960–61	*Jamaica Broadcasting Corporation (JBC)* Announcer

1955–60	*Radio Education Unit, UWI* Secretary to Director of Radio

Film

Children of Babylon	Jamaica
Club Paradise	USA
Glory to Glorianna	Jamaica
Milk and Honey	Canada
Shakespeare on Wheels	Australia
Shattered Image	Jamaica
Small Island	UK
Soul Survivor	Canada
Twenty Thousand Suspects	UK
A Winter Tale	Canada

Stage

The Amen Corner by James Baldwin	Jamaica
Arawak Gold by Carmen Tipling and Ted Dwyer	Jamaica, USA
The Bear by Anton Chekhov	UK
Beyond the Horizon by Roland Reber	Jamaica, Germany
Champagne and Sky-Juice by Basil Dawkins	Jamaica, USA, Canada
Chippy by Sam Hillary	Jamaica
Cinderella	UK
Country Duppy by Aston Cooke	Jamaica, Canada
December by Patrick Brown	Jamaica, USA, Trinidad

Departure in the Dark by Sam Hillary	Jamaica
Double Entry	UK
The Father by August Strindberg	Jamaica
Feminine Justice by Basil Dawkins	Canada, USA
Forbidden by Basil Dawkins	Jamaica, USA
The Gods Are Not to Blame by Ola Rotimi	UK
Hot Flashes by Jean Rhys et al.	Jamaica
I Marcus Garvey by Edgar White	Jamaica, Guyana
The Importance of Being Earnest by Oscar Wilde	England, Ireland
I Thought You Had Gone as Well by Roland Reber	India (World Theatre Project)
A Little Night Music by Stephen Sondheim	Jamaica
Lockdown by Leda Serene	Canada
Maskarade by Sylvia Wynter and Jim Nelson	Jamaica
Miss Unusual by Barry Reckord	Jamaica
Moon on a Rainbow Shawl by Errol John	Jamaica
Mother Courage by Bertolt Brecht	Jamaica
My Son's Friend by Frances Coke	Jamaica
'night, Mother by Marsha Norman	Jamaica
Old Story Time by Trevor Rhone	Jamaica, Canada, Barbados, USA
Oliver by Lionel Bart	Jamaica
The Owl and the Pussycat by Bill Manhoff	Australia
Pot o' Gold by Sheila Graham	Jamaica
The Proposal by Anton Chekhov	UK
Pygmalion by George Bernard Shaw	Jamaica
A Raisin in the Sun by Lorraine Hansberry	Jamaica
Return to Miridal	UK
The Rope and the Cross by Easton Lee	Jamaica, Canada
The Rose Slip by Douglas Archibald	Jamaica

Same Song Different Tune by Basil Dawkins	USA
See Mama by Edward Henry	Jamaica
Smile Orange by Trevor Rhone	Canada
State of Emergency	UK
Stranger Than the Moon by Roland Reber	Jamaica
Toy Boy by Basil Dawkins	Jamaica, USA
The Unknown Woman of Arras by Armand Salacrou	UK
Vicious Circle	UK
Whiplash by Ginger Knight	Canada, USA
A Winter Tale by Leda Serene	Canada
Your Handsome Captain by Simone Schwarz-Bart	Jamaica

Shakespeare:

Antony and Cleopatra	UK
The Merchant of Venice	Australia
A Midsummer Night's Dream	Jamaica
The Taming of the Shrew	Jamaica
Twelfth Night	Jamaica

National pantomimes:

Busha Bluebeard by Louise Bennett and Noel Vaz	Jamaica
Carib Gold by Cecil Nobrega	Jamaica
Ginneral B by Barbara Gloudon	Jamaica
Jamaica Way by Ranny Williams	Jamaica
Pirate Princess by Barbara Gloudon	Jamaica
Queenie's Daughter by Greta Fowler et al.	Jamaica
Sipplesilver by Pat Cumper and Lloyd Reckord	Jamaica
Tantaloo by Gloria Lannaman	Jamaica
Trash by Barbara Gloudon	Jamaica
The Witch by Barbara Gloudon	Jamaica

Television

Jamaica Broadcasting Corporation (JBC)
Jamaica Information Service (JIS)
British Broadcasting Corporation (BBC)
Independent Television (ITV)
Australian Broadcasting Corporation (ABC)

A Graders (series)	Jamaica
Born Free (episode)	USA
Dixon of Dock Green (episode)	UK (ITV)
Going to Extremes (series)	USA
Guttaperc	Barbados
Hope Deferred	Jamaica
Hugh and I (episode)	UK (BBC)
I Is a Long Memoried Woman	UK (BBC 4)
London Line	BBC (for Commonwealth distribution)
Lord Have Mercy (series)	Canada
Me and Mi Kru (series – seasons 1 and 2)	Jamaica
Miranda Hill (pilot)	Jamaica
The Orchid House (4-part miniseries)	UK (BBC 4)
Passion and Paradise	UK (BBC 4)
Pullet Hall (series)	Jamaica
The Seance	Jamaica (JIS/JBC)
Scent of Jasmine	Jamaica (JBC)
Soldier of Fortune (episode)	USA
Songs from the Caribbean (5-minute fillers)	Australia (ABC)
South of the Border (episode)	UK (BBC)
The Stronger	Jamaica (JIS/JBC)
Traxx (series)	Jamaica

What My Mother Told Me	UK (BBC 4)
Winsome Lose Some (series)	Jamaica
Woman under Trial	Jamaica (JIS/JBC)

Other plays and documentaries for BBC and ITV

Nuffield Foundation educational programmes for Africa, Caribbean and
South America

Game shows

JBC/BBC/ABC:

Producer/presenter

News anchor

Hosting morning show, children's programme, woman's programme, light
entertainment programmes

Theatre – producing, directing, acting

Radio

JBC/BBC/ABC:

Continuity

Scriptwriting

Drama productions

News anchor

Outside broadcast commentaries

Radio plays:

Brotherman

Dem Kill Son-Son

The Rope and the Cross

Shadows of the Great House

Sister Angela (soap opera)

What's Good for the Goose

Honours and Awards

Bronze Musgrave Medal, 1973

Order of Distinction – Officer Class, 1980

Institute of Jamaica Centenary Medal, 1981

Silver Musgrave Medal, 1987

City of Kingston Tercentenary Award

Tribute to Excellence, Jamaica National Foundation (New York), 1993

Trophy, Caribbean Academy of Arts and Culture

JBC FM Award for contribution as first Programmes Manager

Lifetime Achievement Award, Caribbean American Theatre
   (West Hollywood, California), 1996

Jambiz Award for Excellence in Theatre Arts, 1999

Jamaica Film and Music Festival, Director's Choice, 1999

Doctor Bird Award, Film and Television, 2000

Actor Boy Best Actress Award, 1991, 1993, 1995, 1999, 2006

Actor Boy Supporting Actress Award, 2001

"Gemini" nominee for *Lord Have Mercy* TV Series (Canada), 2003

Excelsior Alumni Association USA Chapter Award for Contribution to
   Culture (New York), 2004

Prime Minister's Award for Excellence, 2004

Louise Bennett Coverley Award of Excellence (Florida), 2006

Actor Boy Award of Excellence, 2006

Jamaica Festival Gold, Silver and Bronze Medals for Craft

Reel World Film Festival Award for Excellence (Canada), 2006

Best Seller Book Store USA Award for services to the field of
   Theatre and the Arts, 2007

Caribbean Tales Film Festival Award for Excellence (Canada), 2007

University of Technology/Centre for the Arts Award for Outstanding
   Achievement and Contribution to the Cultural Industries, 2011

Press Association of Jamaica Veteran's Award for Distinguished Service to
the Field of Journalism, 2011
Bureau of Women's Affairs, Jamaica 50, 2012
Bigga High Achievers Award, New York, 2012
Proclamations by the Borough of Brooklyn, the New York State Assembly,
the New York State Senate, and Congresswoman Yvette D. Clarke,
United States House of Representatives, 2012

Publications

Moments by Myself, a collection of poems (1988)
Re-Entry into Sound, Part 4, co-authored with Alma Mock Yen (1988)

Plays Written and Produced

De Baby Born – JBC Radio
Let's Say Grace – JBC TV and Radio
One and One Is Three – JBC Radio
What's Good for the Goose – JBC TV and Radio

Appendix 2

‿‿❦‿‿ ‿❦‿‿ ‿❦‿‿ ‿❦‿‿ ‿❦‿‿ ‿❦‿‿ ‿❦‿‿ ‿

From Leonie's Review Scrapbook

The Merchant of Venice

Jamaican-born Leonie Amiel played the finest leading role of Portia that the play has ever seen in Australia.

— *Townsville Daily Bulletin*, 24 May 1969

The Gods Are Not To Blame

The 12 actors surround and act upon Ellen Cairns's drum-skin disc, lit with dramatic variation by Larry Coke. The ensemble work is done effortlessly and the Yoruba songs sound wonderful. In the main individual role, Jeffery Kissoon as Odewale acquires enormous, bull-necked, restless power. His final entrance, on hands and knees, his blood a huge crimson train of cloth reaching back from his head, is a brilliant coup of acting, design and direction. Leonie Forbes, culminating a marvellous performance as

Ojuola, takes one of those knives and moves with riveting, anguished dignity round the circumference to her death.

— The Independent, 21 October 1989

In the commanding point of the stage stands Jeffery Kissoon's King Odewale, asking the questions that will end by driving him blind from his kingdom . . . When he learns the final truth he and the cast (and the theatre, everyone) fall absolutely silent: Kissoon's king cannot bring himself to voice even the sounds of grief. This is a daring and powerful moment, though marginally less tragic than the exit of Leonie Forbes' dignified Queen Ojuola. Her slow walk around the circle, looking in upon the life she is leaving, evokes a heart-catching poignancy.

— The Times, 4 November 1989

MOTHER COURAGE
BY BERTOLT BRECHT
ENGLISH VERSION BY ERIC BENTLEY

The Rope And The Cross

Leonie Forbes is one of the most distinguished actors in the Caribbean and an accomplished broadcaster. Educated in Jamaica and at the Royal Academy of Dramatic Art in London, she has worked in many countries and is internationally acclaimed.

Mervyn Morris is a Jamaican poet and academic. His books include 'Is English We Speaking' and Other Essays and I been there, sort of: New and Selected Poems. He was a theatre reviewer for many years.